ACROSS THE RIVERS OF PORTUGAL

With very best wishes

[illegible]

First published September 1991
by Quest Books (NI)
2 Slievenabrock Avenue, Newcastle, Co. Down, N. Ireland BT33 0HZ.

Typeset by Textflow Services Limited, Belfast.
Printed in Northern Ireland by
The Universities Press (Belfast) Limited

A catalogue record for this book is available
from the British Library.

ISBN 1-872027-04-0

Photographs and illustrations by the author

ACROSS THE RIVERS OF PORTUGAL

BERT SLADER

A journey on foot from Northern Spain to Southern Portugal

QUEST BOOKS (NI)

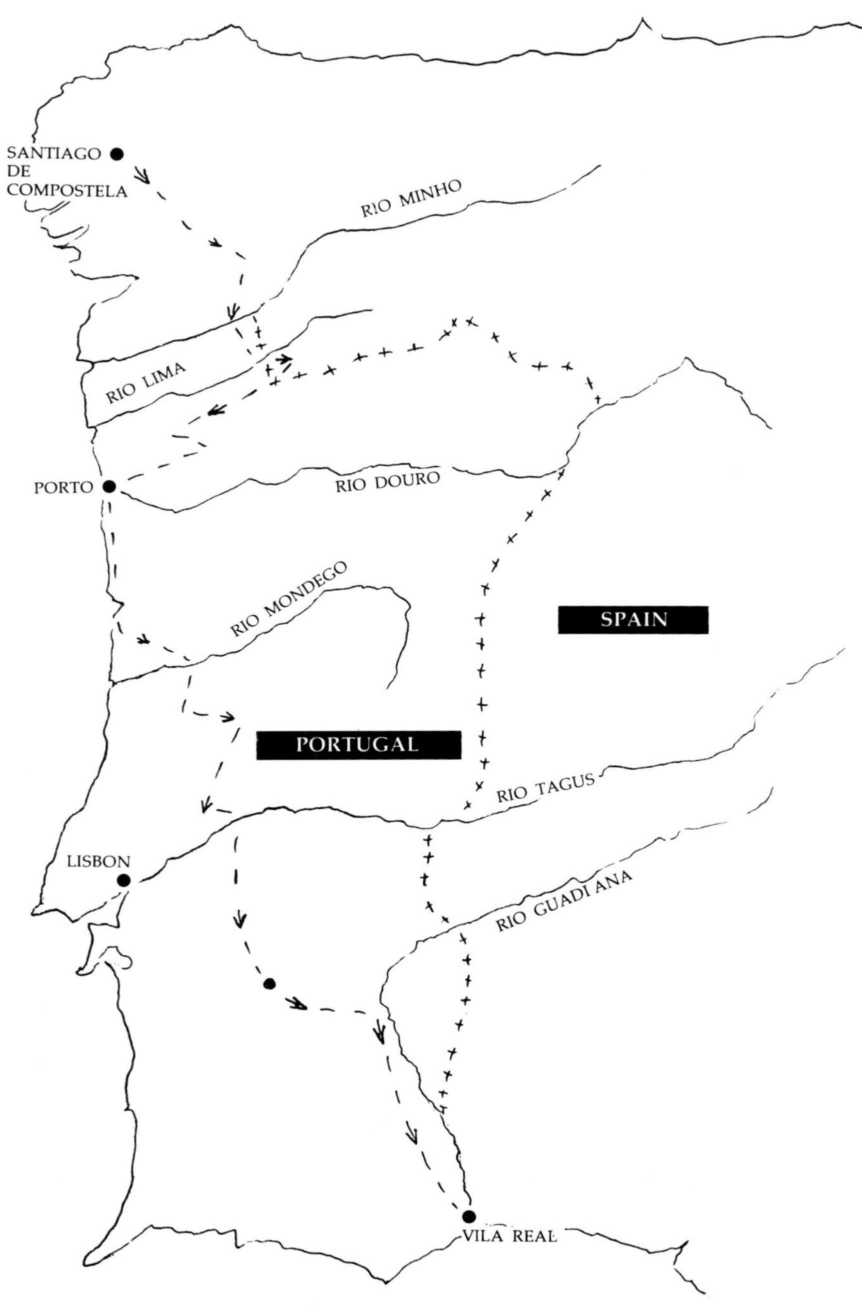

MAP 1 – The route across the Rivers of Portugal

Contents

To those who helped me on the way

I met great kindness on this journey. It was as if the local people understood and accepted my way of travelling. Their help was freely given and at times was crucial to me. I will always remember the retired fisherman and his friends who feature in my 'Tale of the Lost Sole'.

My expatriate friends in Lisbon, particularly Caroline and Jimmy Duff, showed me great kindness and hospitality. They used their knowledge and experience of the country to guide me. Patricia and Norman Wilson smoothed my passage through Porto and Jane Fernandez organised the tram ride in Lisbon and the meal in the Alfalma. I am grateful to them all for their helpfulness and friendship.

The assistance of my family and friends I also freely acknowledge. Their patience and help made this book possible.

My friend Dennis Chambers advised me on the photography.

To those who have encouraged me through their letters and calls, since my first two books were published, I owe my special thanks. Their support gave me a confidence and a freedom of spirit, which made the writing of this book much more for me than a record of my experiences on the journey.

I used 'The Michelin Green Guide, Portugal' published by the Michelin Tyre Company and 'The Rough Guide To Portugal', published by Routledge and Kegan Paul. Both were helpful, accurate and stimulating, and are to be recommended.

My journey 'Across The Rivers Of Portugal' was the second leg of my travels around Iberia. Wherever I went, I was welcomed in the most helpful and friendly way. It was a rare privilege to meet these people and to share their country on my way.

For

Everyone who has travelled with me on other journeys:

On the hills and byways of Ireland and Britain – in Arctic Norway, the Alps and the Pyrenees – on expeditions to the mountains of Turkey, Iran, Afghanistan and the Himalayas – and, most recently, the 65 from Ireland, North and South, who walked with me on my return to the pilgrim road to Santiago this year, to raise funds for the Multiple Sclerosis Charity, MS Ireland.

CHAPTER 1

The Freedom of Wandering

Every momentous journey begins well before the starting point.

It is not the planning, preparations and prior arrangements. They keep the traveller rooted to the spot, necessary, interesting, perhaps even exciting but not the real thing, not the freedom of wandering.

I flew to Portugal to travel to Santiago by train. Near Lisbon long-standing friends, Caroline and Jimmy, entertained me at their penthouse apartment. They talked of Portugal with understanding and perception born of experience and great love of the country. They introduced me to their knowledgeable friends, one of whom was descended from a soldier of Wellington's army who had decided to settle in Portugal after the Peninsular Wars. I heard of the sights, the history, the kindness of the people, the character of the land. I was assured that where ever I went there would always be someone able to help me by speaking English.

The Portuguese train north was fast and efficient but not quite fast enough and I missed a connection at Porto. That evening a slow train shed its passengers in twos and threes stopping at every stop and crawled across the frontier to arrive in the sea-port of Vigo at half past ten.

The station was only partly lit as if there was a black-out in force. Only three of us were left to descend to the platform and, apart from us, the station seemed entirely empty. The others hurried away with the assurance of locals who knew where they were going. As I stepped down I knew there would be no connection to Santiago that night and that I would have to find a bed in Vigo.

Out of the shadow of a pole stepped a fairly tall, lean man, unshaven, stooped, shabbily dressed, furtive. He looked badly worn by the cares of the world, ill-done-by, by fate, expecting and accepting this as his lot.

'¿Quiere una habatacion?' he said 'Do you want a room?' He spoke quietly, conspiratorially, as if he wanted no one to overhear.

I looked him up and down to make sure he knew I was considering him and his offer very carefully. I would like to have said that I 'might' need a room but my Spanish was not up to that.

'Si' I said, 'Quiero una habatacion.' 'Yes. I would like a room.' It was rather more direct and enthusiastic than I wanted to sound, so I shrugged my shoulders as I spoke to indicate that I would have to be persuaded. He looked more doleful than ever and, beckoning me to follow, walked slowly out of the station.

Suddenly he stopped and turned back to me as if he had forgotten something important. He pointed at my rucksac and offered to carry it. I declined the gesture as kindly as I could. To have accepted might have been to commit myself to taking the room, sight unseen and anyway he looked far less able to carry a rucksac than I was.

It contained everything I had with me for the journey but, having carried one in similar circumstances before, it held nothing I could do without. Apart from the camera and tape recorder, my needs were simple and it was relatively light. And luckily so, it would be my daily companion for nearly every one of the next forty days and there is no worse companion than a heavy rucksac. It nags at the back, it pulls at the shoulders, it strains the neck, it chafes the hips. It is at its very worst when the poor traveller is tired and dejected.

Vigo is reputed to be a fine city, one of the premier ports of Spain, set in the middle of a majestic bay. It has a famous historical past illustrated by monuments like the magnificent church of Santa Maria, burned by Drake and rebuilt in Neoclassical style.

But I saw none of Vigo's grandeur on that damp, misty evening as I followed my furtive guide through ill-lit streets near the station. Above a retaining wall there was an open square. My guide led me on a charmed route through the midst of the traffic to an imposing building on the far side. It was a solid, ancient residence constructed of dressed stone, presenting a proud face to the world.

The doorway was huge, the door set back, showing the thickness of the walls. My guide produced a key nearly a foot long, inserted it carefully in the key hole, turned it gently and the massive black door swung open.

The room was on the first floor, clean, comfortable and remarkably cheap.

'Está bien.' I said, indicating that I would take it.

For the first time the doleful look on my companion's face began to fade. Then I asked him where I could eat at this time of the night and he began to smile, very tentatively at first as if he was not used to the experience.

'Tiene una restaurante.' he said 'I have a restaurant.' He was now grinning broadly as he explained that it was just across the square and that he would see it stayed open until I arrived.

We shook hands and parted, almost friends. His head was held a little bit higher, his stoop not nearly so noticeable. I took the keys, a small one for the door of the room and the massive castle-door implement for the front door.

When he left I opened the shutters and Vigo at night, at least the part of it I could see, seemed a pleasant place under the street lights and now that I was on the inside looking out. It only took a matter of minutes to wash and unpack and I locked the front door behind me with that key like a well cut jemmy.

Across the square was a brightly-lit restaurant, smartly painted, expensive-looking, presenting an almost elegant facade to the passer-by. I crossed the road less expertly than my guide but quicker on my feet. As I reached the restaurant I saw that it was indeed a grand place but there was something wrong. It was exactly where my land-lord had indicated his place would be but it was not what I had expected.

It was now well after eleven o'clock and if I did not find a place to eat soon everywhere would be closed. I was beginning to feel confused.

Help, however, was close at hand.

'Senor.' a quiet voice behind me whispered urgently. 'Hola senor.'

I recognised that conspiratorial tone. It was my guide, waiting again for me in the shadows. He led the way down a narrow, concrete ramp beside the fancy restaurant. Underneath the building was a cavern of a room without windows, whitewashed, brightly lit, with fans gently humming to stir the air. There were tables set with cutlery and glasses but no customers. My host showed me to a wooden table with a scrubbed top in the middle of the room.

The woman behind the counter which separated the kitchen from the room, seemed tired, as if she was coming to the end of a long day and could, at last, let her weariness show. I knew that she was my guide's wife. It was the way they looked at each other, not in any loving fashion but with an acceptance of each other that never exists between employer and employee.

She smiled with relief when she heard my order, a Spanish omelette, a basket of bread and a jug of wine. One type of tourist can be disappointed when a simple restaurant fails to provide familiar dishes, like steak and chips, another when no elaborate menu is available. In order to survive, the traveller learns the art of asking for what is possible and dines in style.

As I entered I had seen a notice written in chalk on a black-board. It announced that Tortilla Espãnola was the speciality of the house and at eleven o'clock at night it seemed a most suitable choice for both the restaurant and myself.

When the meal was served my landlord sat down at a nearby table in case I wanted to talk. I told him that I would be taking the train to Santiago in the morning. He smiled understandingly, deferentially.

'You are a pilgrim on the way to Santiago? He spoke in Spanish, his intonation indicating that it was a question needing no answer.

'No.' I said gently not wanting to add discomfiture to confusion. 'Santiago is the beginning, not the end.'

I explained that I had walked to Santiago from France two years before along the Road of St. James. Now I was returning to the Pilgrim city for the next stage south, across the rivers of Portugal.

My landlord and his wife looked at each other and for the first time she spoke.

'Remember us to St.James.' she said with a slow, quiet smile.

It mattered nothing to this couple where I came from. I was a traveller and the only question of interest which occurred to them was where I was bound. I remembered the time when, as a teenager, I had hitch-hiked to the South of France just after World War 2. My companion John and I had met three New Zealanders. They called me 'Traveller Man'. That was forty years ago almost to the month and now I knew what they meant.

The omelette was delicious, smelling of herbs and oil and the chunks of bread and the pale red wine were the perfect accompaniment. My landlord and his wife watched as I ate, enjoying me so obviously enjoying their food.

When I rose to pay and take my leave, and although they were almost certainly younger than I was, it was as if they were parting with a younger relative, a favourite nephew perhaps. It was a strange feeling as if they recognised the energy of youth in what I was doing.

We shook hands and when I stopped at the top of the concrete ramp to turn and wave they were standing together, watching me on my way.

Next morning I travelled with the students by train to Santiago. Although it was very early they were fresher than I would have expected students to be at that time of the day. They were much better dressed too than students at home, not expensively so or formally but casually smart. The cults of slovenliness, of delight in the outrageous had not yet reached this particular university town, or, if they had, had been allowed to pass by unembraced.

My arrival in the City of St. James was of this age, tumbling out of the train with hundreds of other passengers and streaming with them out of the station towards the heart of the city.

Two years before I had arrived on foot after thirty days on the road. It had felt right then, now I was less comfortable. My plan had been to spend a night in Santiago before setting out but the urge to be on the way was too strong. I visited the cathedral and spent an hour or so under the cloisters in the great square before it, the Plaza del Obradorio, watching that great monument to St. James.

It was time to go and I did so in the same spirit that I had begun my journey to Santiago two years before. Then I had faced the Pyrenees, now I was on the pavement of a main road steadily rising from the city. Somehow the much more formidable ascent towards the crest of the Pyrenees Mountains had felt easier than setting out on this urban thoroughfare.

My consolation was that my time would come. Before I left Spain there would be hills to cross. And once into my stride there would be mountains and rivers a-plenty in Portugal.

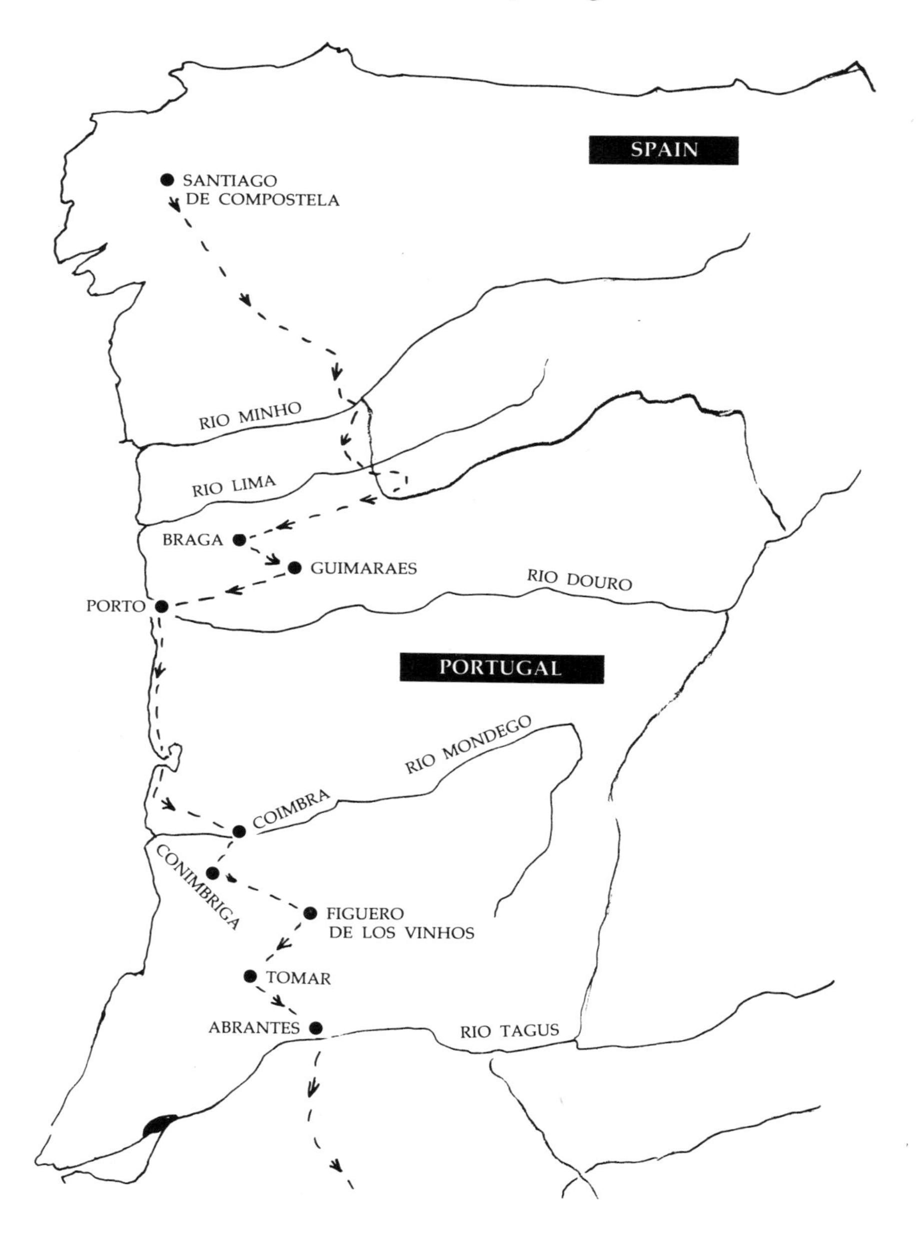

MAP 2 – From Santiago to the River Tagus

CHAPTER 2

From The Pilgrim City

I left the Pilgrim City for the Azure Ocean on my own two feet. It should have been a bright, cheerful leave taking from a place which had such a special niche in my memory – the place where I had finished one great journey and found it a new beginning, not an end. But it was a grey day, like a sea-side town at the end of a bad season, struggling to keep its spirits up against the mist and the drizzle.

A snail on the fancy tiles of the pavement tried to race me on the uphill slope but I speeded up and began to pass him easily.

'Arriba!' I called to him in his own language. 'Arriba! Arriba!'. It was a shout of encouragement I had learned years ago when I met a party of young Spaniards climbing the pass to the King's Lakes in the Pyrenees.

The drizzle turned to rain and I stepped into a shop doorway to let it pass. One mile gone and only another five hundred and ninety-nine to go. But I had six weeks ahead of me for the journey and could spare fifteen or twenty minutes waiting for the rain to ease.

The Pilgrim City is built at the foot of the hills and all roads seem to lead uphill. By the time I reached the outskirts and turned off the main road south towards Portugal, the comforting sunshine of May in Spain was cheering me on my way.

A painted gipsy caravan passed me on the little side road heading north, it was pulled by two fine dun-coloured ponies with three latter-day hippies in the driving seat. A goat rode in state at the back, munching good hay.

I called out a greeting in Spanish and back came an Aussie chorus.

'G'diy'. They roared, 'G'diy sport!' waving and cheering, obviously delighted to be hailed by someone in friendly fashion.

They had to be on their way to Santiago, the last stage of their journey to the Pilgrim City. Meeting them made the day feel right and set me musing.

Santiago de Compostela, the City of St. James, 'the most excellent city of the Apostle . . . the happiest and most sublime of all the cities of Spain.' Amery Picaud, the editor of one of the world's first travellers' guides, published in the twelfth century, had got it right.

Two years before I had arrived there, having followed the ancient pilgrim road from St. Jean Pied-de-Port in France, over the Pyrenees and across the width of Spain to the very north-west corner of that great country.

When I reached the plaza in front of the Cathedral of St. James at the end of that five hundred and fifty mile walk I felt that it was but a pause on a greater journey.

On my return home to Northern Ireland, the first invitation to tell the story to a group had been to the inmates of one of the compounds in the Maze Prison. They had been following reports of my journey and their questions reflected the poignant contrast between their captivity and the freedom of my wandering.

I told them the story of the Belgian boys I had met who had been allowed to walk the Pilgrim Road to Santiago, instead of serving custodial sentences for offences for which they had been convicted. It had been a practice of courts in medieval times and now revived by the legal authorities in Belgium as an alternative to incarcerating young offenders. There were a few wry smiles.

'Bert' said one of the men in the Maze with a slow grin. 'You're a man with contacts in the legal profession. Use your influence and we'll go with you to Santiago any time, no bother at all.'

Later, as I told the story of the journey around the country I knew that I would go back to where I had finished and travel on around the huge peninsula of Iberia.

It seemed obvious that I should start at Santiago de Compostela, the Pilgrim City, and head for the Portuguese frontier. There I would continue south across the rivers of Portugal to the Algarve coast and the azure Atlantic Ocean.

CHAPTER 3

Three Small Kindnesses

By afternoon Santiago seemed so far behind. It was only ten miles back down the road and hard to believe it was but a few hours away in time. Little rain squalls crossed on the wind from west to east, fresh with moisture from the Atlantic, no doubt spent long before the air reached central Spain.

The quiet country road climbed through farmland and forest, a patchwork in shades of green but on a much larger scale than my own country. It was high enough and clear enough after the rain, to let me see to a distant sky-line across woods and streams and lines of low hills.

A man working in the fields beckoned me. His clothes and hat were black and his build stocky. He was in his working coat and trousers but when he spoke, he sounded like a man of property, not arrogant but proud of his land. His farm was well cared for, orderly. It would have been a credit to a farmer of standing in my homeland of Ulster, where such things are prized.

He called me a peregrino and I knew that he thought I was a pilgrim who had walked to Santiago and was now on my way home. He was more than half right but, when I tried to explain that I had travelled to the Pilgrim City two years previously and was now on another stage of my journey, he shook his head in confusion.

'Come and eat with me.' he said, speaking in Spanish, offering hospitality to someone he thought was a pilgrim, and pointing across the neat fields towards his home. But it was in a strange accent, the words lilting against each other like the melody of an Irish jig tune.

I was touched by his offer and should have accepted but there was still a long way to go before I could look for somewhere to stay for the night. There was a feeling too, that by accepting the hospitality when he thought I was a returning Santiago pilgrim, I might be doing so under false pretences.

I thanked him and declined as politely as I could but he look puzzled and disappointed. It was too late now to change my mind. Then I had an idea.

'Portugal' I said. 'Voy a Portugal.' 'I am going to Portugal.'

He brightened up, confusion cleared. For a few moments we talked about that country as he pointed south towards the frontier.

'Buen viaje!' he said, 'Have a good journey.' 'Buen viaje a Portugal!'

He waved, turning as he walked slowly down the path to his home. I headed south with more urgency than necessary, feeling slightly irritated with myself for refusing such a kind invitation. I had missed a chance to talk to this man in his own home, perhaps meeting his wife and family, sharing their lives for a few moments.

Was I deliberately being perverse? I remembered that on the Road to Santiago I had refused a cure for blisters at the first time of asking. But that was out of embarrassment at having the blisters in the first place. Now it might be because of shyness as I was finding the man's Galician accent difficult to understand.

Probably it had most to do with the fact that this was my first day on the road on foot. A sense of urgency dominated all. With forty days to go I was not yet into the stride of the journey. Nearly a week would pass before I could let the route unfold at its own speed, sitting on a hilltop above the view, lingering in an old village where the people would let the traveller be a part of their place, wandering beside a river in a steep valley whose flow measured time on a different scale.

The quest had begun again but I had yet to hear the drumbeat that would carry me at the right pace beyond Spain and across the rivers of Portugal.

I reached a range of hills and, as evening began, came down through vast forests of pine to a village on the main road at the foot of the slope. With twenty-five miles behind me, it was far further than I intended to walk on the first day. The Demon of Urgency had driven me on and now there was no inn when I needed one. I asked three or four people about rooms but they all shook their heads and mentioned the town of Carballino.

In a bar the owner was sympathetic when he saw my disappointment but his message was the same. If I wanted a room I would have to go to Carballino.

'Don't worry.' he said 'The bus will be here in an hour. It's a beautiful town. You'll like it.'

Carballino was to the south-east and I was travelling due south but when I looked at the map, the route from the town to the Portuguese frontier seemed interesting.

I made myself comfortable in the bar and enjoyed talking to the owner and his solitary customer, an old man in well-worn clothes, as aged and dignified as he was himself. When I ordered coffee and a cake the barman brought with them a liqueur, an anisette in a big glass, and the customer nodded politely in my direction.

When it was time to leave I tried to pay but the owner pointed at the customer. The old man smiled to himself, sucked his teeth noisily and opened his coat and waistcoat. He dug deeply into the hidden depths of an inside pocket and with some difficulty extricated a thick wad of notes. He held the bundle close to his face, selecting a note of the right denomination with great care and paid the bill.

A childhood memory spun back to me across the years. My father had been a stud groom and before he came to Ireland had travelled the length of England working at stables. He loved the world that revolved around the horse but when he visited race courses or stayed in town lodgings he guarded whatever money he had with great care.

He showed me a suit, the jacket and waistcoat of which were lined with a specially woven cloth which could not easily be slit with a razor.

He explained that the pick-pockets worked in pairs, one walking ahead of the other. The man at the front would jostle the victim with his right shoulder. At the same time he slit the victim's jacket below the inside pocket with a razor held in his left hand and hidden under his right arm. His accomplice followed closely behind and slid the wallet neatly out of the slit pocket, as the front man apologised to the victim.

If the job was expertly executed, the wallet fell into the second man's hand as he reached for it. They were so skilled the victim felt nothing except the initial jostle and, of course, the later pain of the loss of the wallet.

According to my father the special lining prevented such a coup. When he had to sleep in unfamiliar lodgings he wore his waistcoat fully buttoned on top of his night-shirt, with his wallet safely tucked away in the inside pocket.

Whether my benefactor in the bar in Galicia faced thieves of such cunning I never discovered but it gave him obvious pleasure to treat the traveller from the depths of his pocket. Before I left for the bus I tried to return the hospitality but the old man raised his hands, fingers outspread in polite refusal.

'Para mi, uno solo.' he said, 'For me, one only.'

I shook hands with him and the owner of the bar, feeling in very good spirits in spite of the tiredness. This second small kindness made the long day and the lack of an inn in the village appear of no consequence.

The bus landed me in Carballino in the early evening. It was a small town of great character and charm, ignored by the guide book I had with me and any I have seen since. It was a lively place with interesting streets and alley-ways and a huge medieval church.

I appeared to be the only visitor in town. The locals acknowledged the stranger by smiling in friendly fashion, but not intruding. They waited for me to speak and when I did so were the very essence of helpfulness.

Those who have suffered indignities as tourists on the Costas of Spain would find relief in a place like this. They would feel that they had shared the life of the real Spain.

A comfortable room was easy to find and I ate well in a small restaurant. As I pushed my chair back at the end of the meal the waiter came over with a glass of white, dessert wine, chilled, smelling of freshly peeled fruit. It was a gift from the owner. He stood behind the counter, smiling as I drank his fine wine. It was the third small kindness of the day.

My benefactors could have had no idea of the significance of their generosity. These small acts of true kindness, pressed on me one after the other on my very first day on the road, gave me an inner strength and cheerfulness that carried me, spirits soaring, along the way.

In the morning the Demon of Urgency was still with me. Hurry, hurry, breakfast over, find the way, walk quickly, only two days to Portugal.

Although the day's route was mainly on roads, they were narrow and quiet, over-hung with trees, almost devoid of traffic. They carried me across the hills through great forests of pine and eucalyptus.

A four-foot snake stopped in front of me and fixed me in its stare. Being from Ireland where the last snake was banished from the country by St. Patrick in the fifth century, I was transfixed by surprise. Its markings were elegantly beautiful, designed, I thought, to fascinate when still and make the body invisible when on the move through vegetation. The snake moved first. Curiosity satisfied, it slid away and allowed me to continue.

Flecks of cloud raced across the sky borne on powerful winds I could not feel at ground level. I reached the last crest of the hills and stood amongst pines looking down on the deep valley of the Rio Miño. It was miles below me, one reach as broad as a lake.

To the west, on the far side, a range of mountains met the Miño at right angles. This junction, formed by the mountains and the river, marked in physical form, the north-east corner of the frontier between Spain and Portugal.

Although I had travelled to Spain through Portugal to begin my walk, the first sight of the country through which most of my route lay was a dramatic and compelling moment. It lifted me into the spirit of this new journey.

It was no longer like the Road to Santiago, as if the Pilgrim City had not even been the starting point for this expedition. But why did I still feel like a pilgrim? The journeys must have been connected in some way not revealed to me at the time but part of some inner sense of where I needed to go.

Hours later I walked into the frontier town of Ribodavia, tired and hungry, but easier in myself now that I had seen Portugal from the crest of the hills.

The town was named Ribadavia on the maps but the locals distinctly called it Ribodavia, with an 'o' on the end of the 'Ribo' rather than an 'a'. It is the capital of the wine producing area of Riberio del Avia and, like many a town with a grand past, its people have a proper sense of its importance.

The castle was built in the 14th century and the massive town walls two hundred years before that. The streets are narrow and steep, lined with old buildings faced with fine carved stone work. This town wears its history well.

It was a lively place, particularly around the park and the sports stadium, where the young congregated, a most pleasant town to reach at the end of a day's walk. But both the inns were closed, one for repairs, the other for some reason unknown to the locals.

I found a room above the Bar Caracas. In the evening election excitement spread through the town, as small vans with loud speakers boomed out the candidates' messages. When one van entered a street to harangue the voters another would drive in behind and blow the message away with a great blast of Galician music. When the first van left in disgust, the second would be in no hurry to switch to the message, as if the music was enough.

These Spanish election workers may not have known it but the hippies' guru Marshall McLuhan would have been interested. It is but a short step from 'the medium is the message' to 'the music is the message'.

Next morning I had to steel myself for a day in the same place. In the afternoon I was due to make a telephone link to a BBC radio studio in Belfast and do a live broadcast on my travels so far. This was to be the first of a weekly series to last the length of my journey. By the time the broadcast was over, it would be too late to complete the next stage, to the bridge across the Miño which led to the town of São Gregõrio in Portugal.

I telephoned the studio from a call box and the producer rang me back half an hour later at the Bar Caracas. Just before I went on air I managed to get the barman to turn off a television strategically positioned above my head. But there was no stopping the electronic jangle of the fruit machine. Every few moments its simple, synthesised chords cried out for one more player to feed it with coins and play its buttons for false promises of riches.

I turned my back on it and in a huff it squeaked even louder. Walter Love, the programme presenter and an old friend, greeted me in Spanish. We were on air. As I began to talk about the journey, an election van drove into the street and the message blared out. I knew what was coming. A rival candidate's van was on its tail, with the music at full blast.

Walter is as cool and urbane as broadcasters come.

'We can hear the local music.' he said calmly, 'You seem to be having fun.'

I explained about the election and he was keen to hear which way I was voting. I pleaded the secrecy of the ballot box and we were soon on the much safer ground of my walking experiences so far.

Walter and I battled against the clamour of the fruit machine and the roar of the election music. We managed to talk about the wonderful smell of the eucalyptus trees, the beauty of the broom in bloom, the character and history of this corner of Spain and the three kindnesses I had received along the way.

When the broadcast was over I knew Walter and I had won when the producer held on to the telephone line.

'Great local colour.' he said, 'Live broadcasting should be full of life. Just the sort of spot to do your piece from. Brings the place you're in into the homes of Ulster.'

It may have been nerve-wracking at the time but there was a feeling of exhilaration now it was over. I had a cool glass of wine to celebrate and, in great good humour, spent the rest of the afternoon exploring the town's historical past.

That evening I ate at a restaurant at the other end of town. The waiter recommended the trout, caught locally.

It was served grilled, with pieces of cured ham inserted into slits on the side of the fish. It was the speciality of the house, the waiter told me. He watched me enjoying the red wine of the area, the Riberio. It was light and fresh, served chilled and excellent with the fish.

Over my shoulder I saw a girl come out of the kitchen area. She was tall, in her early thirties, with long copper-blond hair, a physical beauty dressed elegantly in smart-casual style.

She turned towards me and her face was as yellow and wrinkled as dead leaves, deeply lined, the texture of parchment. As she walked across the room she moved as slowly and as stiffly as an ancient invalid. Her face was carefully made-up and her clothing was elegant. At a Paris show, standing still, she could have modelled the height of fashion.

Here she was like an ancient siren. It could only have been illness. No other fate could have been so cruel.

She smiled in my direction, a shy, wan smile.

'Buenas tardes, senorita.' I greeted her as she passed my table.

'Hola, senor.' She replied in the voice of a girl.

She reached the foot of the stairs which led to the staff quarters and set herself for the climb. She gripped the bannister and made it step by step.

The waiter must have seen concern in my face. He shook his head sympathetically.

'She is the owner of all this.' He spoke in his own language and spread his hands wide to take in the fine restaurant. But then there was a note of hope.

'She is a little better than she was.'

The girl had reached the top of the stairs and disappeared from view. She left a feeling of strength behind her, an air of determined purpose, a presence.

Youth and age in the same form. Beauty below the skin. Will the manifestations of age be any easier to accept when we are old?

It was bright and clear when I left Ribodavia early, in the best part of the morning. There was a new spring in my step, a new kind of urgency, not the demon driving me on, but the urgency of expectation. This was the day I should cross my first river into Portugal.

A friendly, portly policeman directed me towards the main road, he was sure it would be easy to hitch a lift.

'Estoy en pie.' 'I'm on foot.' I told him and he looked at me in surprise, as if he had never heard of such a thing, someone wanting to walk to Portugal when there were good lifts going.

I followed tracks and lanes close to the river. It was narrower here, swirling between its banks. The track led to a height and I overlooked the Rio Miño, now in a steep-sided valley, the slopes wooded, bushes down to the river's edge, overhanging the water. The sun glinted on a village on the far side. I could just hear, but thankfully not see, the traffic on the main road, dully rumbling.

Further on the valley opened out and there were farmed fields on the other side. I heard children shouting as they played. Then I saw a man and heard him call to another, fields away, talking to him in a shrill shout. His friend was further away from me but his reply reached across the river on the breeze.

In Ireland some country people take a pride in this ability to shout across the fields to a friend or a sheepdog or a straying beast. It is called 'gowling' in Ulster and not regarded as a very seemly accomplishment in some quarters.

But this Spanish roaring was of a different class entirely. These men were holding a conversation at an extreme distance. It was a skill I was to hear to perfection, if such a skill can be so described, as I travelled through Portugal.

The lane took me through a farm and I saw the vines supported on wires, strung between stone posts. These were thin slivers of granite, four or five feet high, cleverly split and worked to form posts which would last for ever. Since I started it had been a surprise to see that these stone posts were such a feature of the countryside when wood was so plentiful and this was the first time I had seen them used to support vines.

I live below the Mountains of Mourne where granite working is a skilled craft, yet I know of only one field in the whole of the county where similar granite posts may still be found.

I came out on to the road near the bridge over the Miño, where there was a small settlement. A car stopped beside me and the driver was a friendly, middle-aged man, thick-set, talkative. He told me he was a politician, canvassing for votes. We talked for a few moments and, at first, I found him hard to understand because he spoke so quickly.

'Por favor, hablar despacio.' I said, plaintively. 'Please speak slowly.'

He smiled, accepting the stranger's imperfections courteously.

'You have no vote.' he said. 'So, with you, I can be myself.' He smiled, speaking carefully now, with gentle gestures to help me understand.

'Come and have a drink with me.' I detected relief in his voice at this opportunity to stop grafting and talk to someone whose vote he did not have to win.

We sat in a little café and I drank coffee while he sipped a herb tea. Instead of politics he preached herbalism. With his politician's persuasive zeal he explained the evil of caffeine and the virtues of local herbs. It was easy to restrain the urge to tell him that there was no need to talk me into trying herb tea. I lacked the words and, anyway, it would have been ungracious to tell him that I was already a convert.

I nodded, accepting his arguments and smiled. Without having discussed his policies, on the strength of this brief meeting, he would have had my vote.

We shook hands on the steps of the café and he wished me a good journey. On the bridge I stopped half way across and looked down at the swirling water. Without knowing why, I took a small coin from home from my pocket and dropped it into the Miño. It fell edge first and cut cleanly into the river. I fancied I could hear the sharp 'zitt' as it entered.

I walked on over the bridge and the Spanish Rio Miño became the Portuguese Rio Minho.

A little black and white dog came up behind me, growling bad temperedly, and began to bark me across my first river into Portugal.

The Rio Lima – the river of oblivion

CHAPTER 4

Across The River Of Oblivion

I stepped off the bridge into the small, picturesque town of São Gregõrio. It had been long enough for the day and I hoped to find somewhere to eat and sleep here without going any further. The next stage on the morrow would be much longer and across the mountains.

The little shop was so small that I had to take off my rucksac to squeeze inside. I propped the rucksac against the door post and, with my first words in Portuguese, asked the man inside if there was an inn in the town. He looked at me, confused, as embarrassed in trying to understand me, as I was in trying to be understood. I took out my phrase book and tried again but he shook his head in bewilderment.

It was a circumstance I had been dreading from the time I set out on the journey; the need to communicate and the total failure to do so. I tried English, then Spanish and he looked even more perplexed.

For the past few days I had managed quite well, my Spanish is rudimentary but it becomes more fluent as I go. Since I started the only words in English I had heard were the 'G'diy sport' of the Australian latter-day hippies. Now I had need of a few words that would make sense in Portuguese.

I thanked the shopkeeper for trying and backed out of his tiny shop. The little black and white dog knew I was having difficulties. He gave me a cheeky look, lifted a leg and peed on my rucksac. It was only a few drops, but enough to welcome me into his country. He was probably wishing me good luck too.

'Get away with you, you wee divil.' I said to him, with menace but without any ill-feeling.

He smirked, cocking his head on one side and looking at me with one eye. Duty done, he strolled off, back to his station on the bridge. He and I parted on not unfriendly terms. We understood each other.

When I asked other local people about an inn, I met blank stares and shrugged shoulders and began to realise that it was my word for an inn which was causing the problem. I was using the word 'pensão', trying it in different ways, none of which seemed to work. At the edge of the town I went into a gift shop and tried again but this time I showed the woman in charge the word in the phrase book.

'Paynsang.' she said with the last syllable uttered as a nasal sound I had never heard before. Now I understood.

In Ulster we have a way of pronouncing a sound which is not used in other parts of Ireland and so different from standard English, it is often impossible for English people to imitate. It is the 'ough' sound as in the place names 'Clough' or 'Augher', or in 'shough', our word for a ditch. We say 'ough' in the throat, harshly guttural and hard to do unless bred and raised to it. It was easy to accept the right of the Portuguese to their own extremely odd noise.

'Pensão.' I said, trying to imitate the woman's pronunciation. She shook her head and made me repeat it half a dozen times or more until she thought it passable.

She explained that there was no inn in the town but that there was one in Melgaço, not far away. In a few moments she had arranged a lift with a couple in her shop and I was on my way by car.

Melgaço was ten kilometres out of my way and would mean a taxi journey next morning back to my starting point but I felt elated. The kindness of the woman in the shop, the feeling that I could now make a shape at a sentence in Portuguese, and my welcome into the country by the wee black and white dog, cheered me immensely.

The town of Melgaço, too, was a delight. It was early evening when I arrived, the end of a working day. Obviously there had been a market in the huge open centre of the town and the traders and customers from the villages and surrounding countryside were still happily milling around. They filled the cafés and strolled the pavements reluctant to end a day's fun and excitement by going home.

Melgaço had an old-fashioned air, like an Irish country market town in the nineteen forties or fifties, in the days before farming became an industry or farms became factories and the market town was the centre of the world for the whole farming community.

I found the inn without difficulty and arranged for a comfortable room. Later I enjoyed my evening meal in the upstairs dining room, seated at a window table where I could see the stir in the square below.

Again no one I met spoke English. I remembered my Lisbon friends telling me that wherever I went in Portugal there would always be someone who could speak English. I took out my phrase book and did my homework over dinner, asking the waitress to help me with the pronunciation of some of the words.

In the morning a taxi took me back to my starting point and I strolled up a narrow road leaving the farms and villages behind as I climbed. For the first time the route was separating me from the people. The way lay through the range of mountains I had seen two days before from Spain and whose crest marked the frontier.

The peaks were four or five thousand feet high, but they seemed higher because of the long sweep down to the valley of the Minho. This was the Serra da Penada, the mountains I must cross to reach the Rio Lima, The River of Oblivion, my next river of Portugal.

There were Alpine meadows amongst the woods and an occasional wooden shack but, as the morning wore on, no sign of people. The forest gave way to open country amongst the peaks. The first pass was a narrow corridor between cliffs and great boulders, a spectacular setting at the crest of my first Portuguese mountain range.

I paused to enjoy the day and make myself a cup of coffee on my little gas stove. For the first time since leaving Santiago, this day gave me the feeling of being on my own. There was no sign of the ache of loneliness I had carried with me on the Road to Santiago two years before, this time it was simply a feeling of being separated from other people.

Then, the loneliness had been a surprise to me and a mystery. Months afterwards a friend suggested that it had caught me with my guard down, having so much to share and no one to share it with.

Now, I was aware of a physical freedom but the mystical dimension which had been a part of that experience was being revealed in faint glimpses only.

I packed up and walked on across the pass with a prospect of steep wooded valleys and ranges of mountains stretching before me. From here the map made sense but I knew that once I lost height the perspective would be gone and I would need to be in the right valley. I checked the compass and headed almost due south for a river valley which I hoped would lead me to the Rio Lima.

I found myself wondering how others would respond to time in their own company on a long solitary walk. Some might worry about all the chores left un-done, others talk to themselves for company. Some might build castles in the air, day-dreaming of their life's aspirations or, more prosaically, of a great meal and a special bottle of wine at the end of the day's walk.

A few might let their thoughts run free, considering their beliefs or their journey through life so far. There might be those who let their dark thoughts run wild. There might even be some who let themselves enjoy the day sensing the 'la liberté du vagabondage', the freedom of wandering.

I let my spirit run with me, rising with each hill, feeling the effort of the climb, sensing the world that I was passing through, sharing the pain, the excitement of some new view, the comfort of an easy seat against a tree, hope, little pricks of loneliness, un-reasoned sadness, the beauty of the land.

At this moment I remembered the first steps, the walk up the hill out of Santiago on that damp morning which now seemed months ago but was only five days before. I knew now that I had felt like whooping aloud that morning but had been too inhibited to do so. I wondered if I should make up for it in this remote place but decided that it would not be fair to startle the wild life. Amongst the vastness of this natural beauty it was more comfortable to let the spirits do the cheering.

Miles later I found the head waters of the tributary of the River Lima and began to descend with it. Then the track had to turn away as the little river dropped into a steep gorge. It took me west across a ridge and into another valley but instead of following this valley down towards the Lima, the path led upwards back the way I had come. I realised that this enabled it to cross the valley at its head and then follow the river down on the far bank.

It might seem an obvious move to leave the path in such circumstances and cut across country. It is rarely a good tactic. On the open mountain the walker can choose his or her own route. In this lower part of the valley, chock full of prickly bushes and thorn thickets, it is essential to stick to the path.

The afternoon heat made the going hard. Half an hour later I was back down the valley on the other side, level with where I had started. Then the track crossed another ridge and, to my annoyance, the same prospect of trekking up the valley to cross at its head, faced me again. But this time there was something to cheer me. I could hear music, surges of happy sound rising towards me.

Far below in the steep valley a little hillock stood out above the trees and perched on top of it was a tiny village. As I watched I heard fireworks and saw rockets shoot skywards, exploding with multi-coloured stars almost level with my perch. It was a strange experience to have these missiles rise up from the depths of the valley and burst before me as if specially arranged for my entertainment.

It had to be a wedding and although I could see nothing but the tiny roof tops I could hear the happy laughter and the music. I rejoiced with them and wished the couple well.

The music had an intonation I had never heard before, a lilting, singing guitar behind a woman's voice. It wafted up the valley to me on the wind, rising and falling in the air.

I learned later that this was the fado, the sad, compelling song descended from the airs of the troubadours of the Middle Ages. The name is derived from the latin 'fatum' or destiny and the song is accompanied on the guitarra, the Portuguese guitar. The guitarra has twelve metal strings, set in pairs and capable of the subtlest of airs and at its finest accompanying the fado.

My journey through Portugal was to the sound of the fado. The further I went the more it became a part of my experience of this exciting and unusual country.

Although my track was once more playing the same trick as before and requiring me to go back the way I had come and cross the valley at its head, I was now in good form, too cheerful to let it disappoint me.

I found a tiny path down through the trees to the river. It was easy enough to wade across and, on the other side, were farmed fields and a village I had not been able to see for the trees. I climbed the bank on the far side towards the track and came out at the village bar.

It was a small success but it had saved a half hour of walking time and needed to be celebrated. I had a cold drink and strode on.

Ten hours after leaving Melgaço I came out of a pine forest at the top of a cliff and looked down on the Rio Lima hundreds of feet below.

It was a magnificent sight. The Lima has the reputation of being the most beautiful river in all Portugal. I could believe it. The Romans thought it so. The travel guides recommend it. Here, I was above it and weary after the day's walk, but its magnificence stopped me in my tracks.

The Lima is in a deep, deep valley between two great ranges of mountains. It is on the grand scale, wooded, the sinuous twists of the river cutting into the very floor of the depression. The Spanish frontier is close by, hugging the crests of the mountains to the east.

When the Roman legion first reached the Rio Lima, on the conquest of this part of Iberia, the soldiers believed it was the Lethe, the mythical River of Oblivion, of Forgetfulness. They approached from the south and in spite of the urgings of their Consul, Decimus Brutus, stopped at the water's edge and refused to cross.

Their poets and those of the Greeks before them had taught that the river water had the power to make the traveller forget home and country. Once on the other side, the Elysian Fields, they would live in charmed serenity, oblivious of their past lives and never to return whence they came.

The Consul seized the standard and forded the Lima. On the far bank he called his soldiers to him by name and one by one they crossed to his side, reluctantly, but drawn to him by loyalty and legionaire tradition.

I wondered what effect the Lethe would have on me. I would be crossing in the other direction, from north to south, leaving the Elysian Fields for the real world. Would it bring me into closer harmony with my homeland.

The map showed that the bridge was some way down stream but work was in progress on a dam across the river and I could see another bridge had been constructed to facilitate this. It was directly below me, a long way below me, but much nearer than the bridge down stream.

Descents feel as hard as ascents on tired legs and I wound my way down on workmen's tracks. The bridge was a temporary affair but I stopped in the middle and looked down at the waters of the Lima, savouring the moment. Again without knowing why, I dropped a coin from home into the flowing water and made a wish, a wish that had to stay secret to be fulfilled.

It was now well into the evening but the heat was still trapped in the valley and I sweated and struggled up a steep track to the main road above.

I turned to look back across the valley to the mountains of the Serra da Penada, behind me now, rugged and formidable. I remembered the Roman legionaires and imagined them travelling north over these hills, along the way I had come from the Minho

From the map the village of Lindoso appeared to be near at hand and I asked a young man about an inn. He shook his head and pointed down the valley, mentioning the name of a town which was well off my route.

A second man was sitting in the porch of his house and he was much more encouraging. He pointed to a lane opposite and I gathered that it led to the inn. It often helps to have a second opinion.

The lane led to a large open area at one end of the village. The houses were built of granite, fitted into the landscape as if they were meant to be part of it.

On a hill to my right was the castle and below it a group of granaries like Spanish hórreos but built of granite rather than wood. They are still in use and there must be fifty or more of them standing together like monuments in a cemetery.

The castle faced the armies of Philip 4th of Spain when Portugal had to fight for independence in the 17th century. The keep is surrounded by great bastions and turrets and the field of view across the Lima and the frontier with Spain must be spectacular.

I had, however, a more urgent call than the view from the castle watch tower. It was eight o'clock on a Sunday evening, I was tired and hungry, and had a long day across the mountains ahead of me. Rest, recuperation and sustenance must take precedence over the most interesting historical or cultural sights. I needed a meal and a bed for the night.

Standing on its own to my left was a solid, whitewashed, two storey building with a flight of stone steps at one end leading to the upper storey. It looked like a Devon long house, set amongst these rugged Portuguese hills.

It had to be the inn. Perhaps the young man I had first asked had felt I would require more salubrious quarters in some hotel. It was easy to tell from the noise that the bar was doing good business. As I entered, the small room was packed with excited locals enjoying their Sunday evening out. The throng parted for the stranger without request, politely, even deferentially, as if the traveller was an aristocrat of the church.

The man in charge was in his thirties, dark, dour, not a man to try to engage in casual conversation.

He acknowledged my halting request for a room by half closing one eye under its bushy black eyebrow and slightly tilting his head forward. He ducked under the counter and motioned to me to follow. We went outside and I saw that he had a limp, one leg perfect, the other deformed. He was under medium height, stocky, powerfully built and he moved his shoulders as he walked to balance his bad leg.

In Ireland such a man might still be called 'brougie'. At the foot of the Mourne Mountains there is a pub called 'Brougie's' even though the man who gave it its name is long gone. He hated the nickname and he too was the same strong, stocky build. A man who could look trouble straight in the eye, limp or no limp.

No one had ever been heard to utter the nickname in his presence unless well taken in drink or knowing no Irish and thus having no idea of the significance of the word. The former he treated firmly, even vigorously on occasions, as he showed them to the door. The latter he excused with a hard, mirthless smile and a fool's pardon.

My host climbed the stone steps slowly and uncomfortably and we entered the upper storey of the inn. The corridor was untidy, unswept. The paint was peeling from the walls, the plaster flaking. Through an open door I saw the chaotic interior of a room. It was piled with stores, strewn with rubbish, cardboard boxes on the bed, opened cartons spilling their contents on to the floor. I looked away, pretending to myself that I had seen nothing out of the way.

My host reached a room and opened the door. It was neat and clean, with a large old-fashioned bed topped by brass bed-posts. There was a marble wash stand and an enamel basin and jug. A small window, set into the deep walls of the inn, looked out across the mountains. It was in total contrast to the dirt of the corridor and the squalor of the other room.

As I agreed to take the accommodation, there was a great crash of thunder to tell me I had made a timely choice. The rain began in a torrent, big drops dashing against the window panes. The mountains disappeared behind a curtain of streaming mist. My host left, telling me gruffly that I could eat now.

'O jantar! Agora!', 'Dinner! Now!'. He spoke loudly, not as an order but more of a friendly warning that, unless I came now, there might be none left.

It took only moments to unpack and dash down the stone steps through the storm and into the dining room, beside the bar.

Inside, the wooden trestle tables were arranged in a row, crowded with customers, but the locals welcomed me and vacated one corner for the visitor.

I had a huge plate of soup, just what I needed after the long walk. Then a girl brought me a large casserole of delicious lamb stew and a jug of red wine. The storm raged outside, the customers chatted happily. I dipped chunks of bread in the stew and sipped the wine and felt I was in the most hospitable inn in Europe.

The locals wanted to talk to me but, if I had only a few words of their language, they had none of mine. Then I discovered that most of the men could speak some French. It was a heavily accented patois, but French none the less.

They told me that the men of the area went to work in France for a part of the year to earn good wages and to bring the money home. It had a familiar sound. In many a county of Ireland such a seasonal migration was, and in some places still is, a vital part of the rural economy. The men would work the winter in Scotland or England or America and come back in the summer to fish, to farm and to ensure that there was another mouth to feed next year.

I was enjoying the chat, the food and the wine, but it was obvious that they intended to make a night of it and it was time for me to rest. I stopped in the shelter of the door-way at the top of the stone steps and watched the storm flashes behind the castle. No 'Son et Lumière' show could have competed but I hoped it would be spent by morning.

My room felt strangely familiar, as if I had been staying here for weeks. I undressed and was asleep before my head reached the pillow.

CHAPTER 5

Red Revolutionaries on The Roman Road

Although it had been a late night, the bar of the inn was open early. I had a large milky coffee and some stale buns for breakfast, both tasted great.

It was still raining when I left, not like the downpour of the previous evening but I had the feeling that there was a day's steady rain in front of me.

I left the road for a track I had spotted on the map, which I reckoned would take me right across the mountains of Peneda Gerês. As I paused to check the map again, a car stopped and, when the driver wound down the window, I saw that he was a policeman. He pointed at the track and shook his head.

'Sentido proibido.' 'No road.' he said sternly.

I leaned into the car through the open window to keep the map dry as I showed it to him. He recognised the features as his finger traced the route and he read the names. But he dropped the corners of his mouth and shook his head again.

'Sentido proibido!' he said loudly, in the form of an order.

I was sorry now I had paused to let him talk to me, so I smiled, thanked him and began to move off up the track.

The rain was heavier now but he jumped out of the car, ran around to the passenger side and opened the door. What he said, I did not understand but I knew what he meant when he pointed at the passenger seat. He was ordering me to get into the car.

It was pleasant enough being driven through the heavy rain but where was he taking me? He pointed ahead and looked at me in almost friendly fashion now he had me in custody.

'Espanha.' he said, confidentially.

In a few moments we reached the frontier and he drew up beside the Portuguese post. He shook hands with me and pointed across to the Spanish post. With no idea why I was being deported from Portugal, I began to walk towards Spain – at least I was free again.

I heard a shout behind me. It was my former captor and he was pointing towards the range of mountains which formed the natural frontier.

'O caminho.' he roared. It was like the Spanish for a path that I thought he might be directing across the mountains, but on the Spanish side.

I waved back to him and walked into Spain in the rain. It was still raining when I reached a tiny hamlet half an hour later. It was completely closed, no one to ask about the way now I might be able to make myself understood. I checked the map and headed for the hills up a narrow track. It climbed steadily, the weather far too wet to think of stopping after a couple of hours to boil water for coffee on my little gas stove.

The rain eased for an hour when I reached a wood and the birds entertained me as I had tea and two biscuits for lunch. The ridge was crossed easily but it was a most tortuous route down into the next valley. It began to feel like a very long day when the rain began again in earnest.

Once out on the road I had to turn back towards Portugal, tired, hungry and in the lowest of spirits since Santiago. It seemed such a long way around but at least the pass crossed by this road should take me directly to the hill town I was heading for that night.

I passed a bar but it was closed and shuttered. Dogs came out of a lane-way from a farm and barked in a most unwelcoming way. I looked in the rucksac to see if I had overlooked any items of food but there was nothing left but one broken chocolate biscuit, with little pieces of fluff adhering, lurking at the bottom of the bag. It tasted good once unpicked of fluff.

I was within a couple of miles of the head of the pass when it began to rain again, the whole valley filled with driving squalls. There was no shelter, not even a verge to walk on.

Out of the deluge a little car came struggling up the slope behind me and stopped a few yards ahead. One of the smallest men I have ever seen jumped out of the passenger side and ran back to me.

'You speak German?' He said in Spanish. 'You speak French? English?'

In spite of the downpour I managed to smile at the sight of this tiny man, jumping about in excitement, as if to dodge the rain drops.

'English.' I said. 'I'm not English but I speak it.'

He grabbed me by the sleeve of my anorak and and pulled me towards the car.

'Come with us to the pass.' he shouted. 'We have much room.'

It was good of him to ask but the little car was full, three adults in the back and only the front passenger seat free. He pushed me into it rucksac and all and packed himself in beside me, almost climbing on to my knee so that he could slam the door.

'We are Portuguese.' he said, 'Going to the frontier to protest.'

The driver grinned at me, wiped a small patch of the windscreen free of condensation and coaxed the little car up the hill.

The tiny man spoke English without inhibition, obviously enjoying the new audience provided by the stranger.

'Are you from America?' he asked leaning forward so that he could see my face.

'No.' I said 'I come from Ireland, from Northern Ireland.'

'From Ireland!' he shouted, almost dancing on his perch between me and the door. He banged the roof of the car with his fists and translated for the benefit of his friends.

'Up the IRA!' he roared slapping me on the back. 'Up Sinn Fein!' He was jumping up and down making the car rock. His friends grinned tolerantly.

'The IRA are our friends.' he said. 'We meet them in Barcelona. We are communists. We are freedom fighters.' He punched his clenched fist at the roof of the car. 'Up the IRA!'

'James Joyce! Gerry Adams!' he roared obviously expecting me to appreciate his intimate knowledge of Irish literature and politics. What a juxtaposition of names. The writer who revolutionised Irish writing and the revolutionary whose party is dedicated to re-writing the political history of Ireland with a gun in one hand and a ballot box in the other.

The driver was a large man, bulky, black bearded, like an amiable anarchist of the thirties. He waved a hand to calm the little man, but he was too agitated to be put down that easily.

'In Ireland you meet IRA men?' he asked.

I looked at each of them to see their faces, turning to view the three in the back.

'Yes.' I said after a suitable pause, 'And UDA and UVF men.' He obviously recognised the initials of the two most prominent Protestant para-military organisations in Northern Ireland for he sat back towards the door, trying unsuccessfully to shrink away from me.

I smiled bleakly and explained that I had met members of all three organisations in the Maze Prison. The Maze was obviously another word familiar to the little man. He relayed the information to his friends.

There was a silence in the car which even he was reluctant to break. We listened to the rain beating down on the roof, the swish of the windscreen wipers and the agitated drone of the over-worked engine. My tiny companion and his friends were thinking it over.

I could have gone on to explain that I had been to the Maze, at the invitation of the inmates and the authorities, to take sports' leader training for long-term prisoners in all three of the famous compounds. However, I decided to leave things as they were.

Suddenly we had arrived. The sturdy buildings of the frontier post emerged from the mist, guarding the head of the pass.

For the first time the driver spoke.

'We stop here.' he said and parked the car well short of the Portuguese border police.

The rain had eased and they all got out to shake hands with me. The little man danced around us, hardly able to contain himself now we had arrived for the protest. The driver spoke again.

'We are not allowed into our own country.' he said, without emotion or explanation.

I wished them good luck and walked towards the border crossing.

'Up the IRA!' the little man shouted at my back when I was twenty yards away. 'Up the IRA! Up Sinn Fein!'

I turned around and the others were bundling him back into the car. That done the driver shrugged his shoulders at me with his arms spread wide, as if to say . . .

'Forgive us, friend. We can do nothing with him.'

As if to welcome me back, the rain eased as I crossed into Portugal. The solid weight of cloud that had been draped over the mountains all day began to lift. It changed in colour from the dullest, deepest grey to a hopeful greyish-white flecked with white, and in texture, from the dense matt of a damp army-blanket to fluffs of sheep's wool caught in a hedge.

A shaft of sunlight hit the wet road in front of me and I hurried to step into its warmth. It followed as I strolled downwards, keeping me in its beam, the first sunshine of the day and a tonic that could not have been matched by the praise of men or the contents of any bottle, medicinal or otherwise.

My anorak dried in a few moments and I stowed it in my rucksac. My legs warmed up for the first time since I had left the inn. Now I was pleased that I had walked in shorts to keep my trousers dry, on the sound but stoic logic that the skin of my legs would be more waterproof than the special airlight fabric of my Rohan trousers.

I looked back at the pass, the Portela de Homen, and remembered that this was the route of an ancient Roman road. It connected the city of Braga in northern Portugal through the pass and across Spain and France to Rome itself. On the way it passed through Astorga in northern Spain, a fascinating town which had been on the route of my previous journey to Santiago.

The Roman Empire was built by the army. The legions had to be mobile to reach its outposts and the roads were constructed to hasten their journeys. The soldiers were expected to cover long distances each day, carrying full kit.

To be fit for walking and fighting they trained hard on a three-day cycle. On day one they did a forced march, probably at jogging speed and carrying heavy gear. On day two they worked hard, cleaning and repairing equipment and doing camp chores. Day three was a rest day and day four was the beginning of the next cycle. As a training schedule for their role as mobile fighting men, it would be hard to better, even with the benefit of the most up-to-date scientific fitness techniques.

For journeys such as theirs or mine, a training programme is to be strongly recommended.

Having met the legionaires in spirit on the previous day, when I crossed the River of Forgetfulness, this was another moment when I felt not quite of this time, but in some mystical way linked to those hardened travellers who had made their way across this pass two thousand years ago.

I was now back in the National Park area of Penada-Gerês and it was the most beautiful terrain. The sunshine probably helped and I wandered down through natural woods, first of fir, then of oak, eucalyptus and cork oak with hydrangea bushes right down to the roadside. There were great peaks behind steep-sided gorges, and glimpses of streams in deep clefts, the water glittering and sparkling in the light.

At the first National Park sign there was a wooden shack, closed but with a grand place to sit outside it in the sunshine. A sign indicated that there were deer and wild horses in the park.

As I boiled water on my stove for a cup of coffee, a Range Rover pulled into the parking area near me. It was the first vehicle I had seen since entering Portugal at the pass and it had a GB sticker on the back. The driver parked and the family alighted to prepare for a picnic. There were three adults and three teenage children, all in good form, talking loudly, laughing and jesting with each other.

As they set out the food, and presumably because there were no deer or wild horses in evidence to make this beautiful spot even more exciting than it was, they began to discuss the travelling man cooking on his little stove.

My hearing is exceptionally keen, a fact I had discovered as a young teacher and which had proved as valuable to me then as rifle microphones are to undercover agents now. In those days I could hear whispered conversations at the back of the class and was much better informed than the pupils would ever have expected their teacher to be.

Although the picnickers were twenty or more yards away and thought they were talking quietly, their sharp voices carried and I could hear the conversation distinctly. They were talking about me, so I had no conscience about listening.

'He's obviously French.' said one of the women in a large floppy sun hat and in that upper-class southern English tone that neither expects nor intends to brook any argument.

'Expect he's up from Porto for a day in the park.' said the man. It was in a much more tentative, speculative tone as if, as usual, he wanted to be pleasant and helpful.

'Hardly very safe – him wandering about on his own.' said the other woman, safe herself in the security from the elements of very large designer sun glasses and a card sharp's eyeshade. 'Perhaps he doesn't realize how wild and rugged these hills really are.'

It was strange to be sitting at my ease drinking a cup of coffee and being discussed so frankly by these picnickers. It had been a long time since breakfast and I was tempted to go over and pretend to be French to try to cadge some food.

Discretion, however, prevailed. I had a feeling that real travellers like this crew would be fluent in every European language including Polish and Serbo-Croat and probably spoke French better than the French. Me trying to pretend to be Jean-Paul on a walking tour would have been as obviously a fraud as an American actor playing an Irish priest, in an Australian film I saw some years ago and giving the game away every time he said the word Drogheda.

I finished my coffee and stood up to pack my gear into the rucksac. As I turned and hefted the sac on to my shoulder, the three teenage girls were giggling.

'Well I think he has very nice legs.' one of them said firmly, 'Foolish to be on his own or not.'

'Fair enough.' said the woman in the big designer sun glasses and the card sharp's eyeshade. 'Very young legs – for a man of his age.'

She laughed and the others joined in.

I was ready to go, so I bowed and raised my sun hat and treated them to my most winning smile. Every little bit of encouragement helps along the way and to hear that I had what looked like young legs under me, with five or six hundred miles in front of me, was a great comfort.

Behind me there were startled squeaks as if they now realised that I had heard and understood. I turned and waved to reassure them that we were parting friends, even though we had never met. They all waved back, the girls and the women cheerily and the man in a more tentative, speculative way as if, as usual, he wanted to be pleasant and helpful.

The stroll downhill to the spa town of Gerês was idyllic even though I was tired and hungry. I passed the camp site at the edge of the town, beautifully terraced with geometric beds of flowers in full bloom and an air of being exceedingly well maintained. But not a tent to be seen, not even one small hiking tent, although it was the month of June.

The town itself was elegant in a rather old-fashioned way, clean streets, freshly painted buildings, ready for the summer season. It was an immediately relaxing and hospitable place. I made up for my day's near-fast with an omelette and a glass of wine, followed by my first taste of Portuguese cakes.

These pastries were so good I cunningly resolved to make sure I had a substantial ration of them every day. It would help me combat the kind of weight loss which I had suffered after the first two weeks of my walk to Santiago. Then I had used much more energy walking than I had made up through my daily meals. Now I intended to redress the balance, in the most appetising way, by keeping myself well supplied with patisseries.

The main street had a row of charming, Victorian hotels, complementing each other in grandeur, using their collective support to keep up the old standards. But then this impressive facade was only to be expected in a spa town famous for its waters for the past 150 years.

I found an inn at the bridge and it was of the same epoch. The huge hallway was also a sitting room and the television was directly over the reception desk. The late afternoon crowd were in serried ranks watching a programme, women in hats clutching handbags on their laps, men bare-headed, their caps hanging on the hat rack at the door. The heads turned as I entered and I was nodded across to the desk by the massed ranks of the patrons, heads turning in unison like spectators at a tennis match.

My room was off a grand interior balcony and it was as comfortable a haven as could have been wished for by the traveller. The whole place was like a working museum, allowing me the privilege of staying a night in the past, and in some style.

Many of the fitments dated back to the early years of the century, like the brass water taps in the wash-hand basin and the lavatory flush mechanism, but every item so well maintained that it was in perfect working order. Only the telephone and the television were the obvious exceptions, as if to prove the rule.

I ate well at a table overlooking the river and resolved to come back to this town to spend the longer time it deserved. Had it come much later on my journey the temptation to linger might well have been irresistible.

In the morning I was away early and found myself descending gently on a quiet road through a most beautiful and spectacular part of the National Park. There were high peaks on the skyline and little farms and hamlets hiding between wooded hills. The road was cut into the bank above a long, narrow lake, flanked by shrubs in bloom and set into the heart of this captivating countryside.

I saw a camper van through a gap in the bushes, parked on a patch of grass overlooking the lake. There was a NZ sign on the back and the debris of a meal in the open air scattered around. Four young men, in various stages of sleepiness, as casual and untidy as their kit, were having breakfast, eating as if by memory, from dixie lids. I had missed the chance of a conversation the previous afternoon when the Range Rover parked near me, so it was time to take the initiative.

I spoke quietly lest the shock of wakening would be too much for these lads.

'Bom dia.' I said without thinking and being used to greeting people I met in the language of the country.

'Hi.' One of the lads looked up and spoke to the stranger but without expression or encouragement and went back to his food.

Uncharacteristically for me, I persevered. I found that these four young New Zealanders were on a three-month tour of Europe. They had been working in London to earn enough for the trip, bought an ancient mini-bus and crossed the Channel to France. That country had been a disappointment – so had Northern Spain. They had not liked the cities and had been amazed and disillusioned when they found that no one seemed to speak English.

Only two weeks into the journey and it was beginning to feel like a big mistake. The only hope, as one of them said, was that the next place would be more interesting. It was the hope of something better that had kept them travelling. That was until the previous evening.

After making a meal they had gone to the nearest village for a drink and found all the local young people gathered in the bar to watch the football match on TV. Sporting Lisbon were playing Porto and the fans had turned up in their club colours, the young men in hats and scarves and the girls in club jerseys.

It had been a great night with beer and wine, and roaring and cheering, and exciting action on the TV screen. The New Zealanders had taken sides diplomatically, two for Lisbon, two for Porto. Although none of the locals spoke English and they spoke no Portuguese it had been a marvellous evening. As they re-lived the fun, the lethargy of the morning-after-the-night-before dropped away and suddenly we were friends.

I told them about my journey and they knew that I understood about theirs. The travelling men had met.

They were interested in my walk to Santiago and had driven along some of the route. I told them about my weekly broadcasts to Northern Ireland from where ever I happened to be. They were shy about being interviewed on tape, then the youngest volunteered and they all had a turn. The process of recording intrigued them and seemed to concentrate the minds. It was a challenge and it roused them from slovenly ease, without pain, to sharp witted action. We talked about their work as porters at the British Museum and their journey so far. They enjoyed the telling.

I knew that, had I been making my journey by car, we would not have been able to have this conversation. The age gap would have suffocated it at birth.

Young people need time to find the way themselves without someone telling them how to do it – freedom to learn by doing, even by making mistakes – time to rebel against conventional ideas – freedom to learn to live within the law – like teenagers becoming adult because their parents or teachers allow them to take responsibility for what they do.

It has to be sufficient responsibility at the right time, not too much too soon, or too little too late. If we want to stay involved we must find ways of staying in contact with the young, sharing ideas and experience, not on our terms, or even on their terms but on terms with which we are both comfortable.

If we lose contact with the young, we lose contact with the future.

When I walked on I left four friends behind, knowing that, even though we were taking different routes through Portugal, we would meet again. It had happened with the Belgian boys on my Santiago walk and it seemed bound to happen with these four New Zealanders.

Bom Jesus

CHAPTER 6

The Celtic Village on the Hill

The way led delightfully down to a confluence of rivers, dammed above and below where I crossed, at the meeting of the waters. It was after mid-day and time to eat. I found an idyllic place for lunch on a little hillock overlooking the upper dam and shaded by eucalyptus trees. I could see across the lake for miles, to the spot where the New Zealanders had camped and wondered if they were still there, struggling with preparations for their mid-day meal.

The afternoon saw me out of the park and the tiredness came earlier, having covered over 45 miles on the previous two days. When I came out on a main road, I felt I had walked far enough and found that the last bus of the day was due in half an hour's time. It took me to Braga, my first city since leaving Santiago and now a week since the walk began.

Braga was the size a city should be, big enough to be aware of its own importance, small enough to be accessible. It was founded as Bacara Augusta by the Romans in the 3rd century BC and was one of their most important towns in Western Iberia. Now it is the capital of the Minho Region and has a liveliness and charm, dignified by a rich, ecclesiastical heritage in its architecture. Many regard it as the religious heart of Portugal.

Although the evening was a solitary one for me, without conversation or even one word exchanged in my own language, I felt comfortable in this little city. After a good dinner, I strolled the ancient streets, feeling part of the throng. When I stopped in a bar for a glass of port, and without speaking a word to anyone, I was part of the company. The port was white and served chilled, a most charming and elegant drink.

Next day I took a bus to the edge of the city and reached the great monument of Bom Jesus do Monte in mid-morning. Once again on a journey I found myself approaching a religious shrine without knowing why I was making the visit.

Bom Jesus was on my way, of course, and meant to be one of the most impressive monuments in Portugal. It is a sacred shrine which draws pilgrims from all over the country. But, whereas Santiago's significance stretches back many centuries before the Reformation, Bom Jesus was built in the 18th century by the Archbishop of Braga. Is it a manifestation of Catholic adoration whose meaning may only be understood by true followers of the Church of Rome?

Bom Jesus is built on a hill, perhaps four or five hundred feet high. The summit is crowned by a magnificent Baroque church and, leading from the bottom of the hill to the top, is a huge ornamental stairway constructed of carved granite and decorative plaster. It is cut into the wooded slopes, and stands with the church at its head as one massive edifice . . .

Bom Jesus was conceived as a grand allegorical pilgrimage. The pilgrims ascend the first flights, 'The Stairway of the Five Senses', then 'The Stairway of the Three Virtues', passing tableaux showing scenes from the life of Christ. These lead up the hundreds of steps to the Crucifixion at the altar in the church.

There was no one around to see me start at the bottom, slightly sheepishly, wondering whether I was a tourist or a pilgrim. Half way up I met an elderly Portuguese couple descending.

'Is it far to the bottom?' the man asked, first in Portuguese and, when I failed to understand, then in French. The man patted his heart as if he was worried about himself.

'Not far.' I said. 'Go easily.'

I climbed slowly, aware that this ascent was only one step farther on a long day ahead. I passed no one, once out of sight of the Portuguese couple the great staircase seemed empty. I had read of its popularity, devoted pilgrims thronging the steps, sometimes climbing on their knees. But on this day, there was no one going either up or down.

Then, near the top, I heard the clamour of voices and I came out on a grand balcony in front of the church to find the place thronged with people. The reasons for the empty stairway were immediately evident. The tour buses were parked in a neat line to the left of the church and there was an ancient hydraulic funicular, its workings hidden in the woods to one side of the stairway, quietly and secretly raising customers to the summit.

In a way it was a disappointment to find these modern pilgrims avoiding the pilgrimage, reaching the end the easy way. On my previous walk, the Pilgrim Road to Santiago, I had been there for the journey and found myself becoming a pilgrim as I travelled. The city of St. James had been a new beginning, not an end in itself.

Here, I wondered if this great allegorical shrine had become somewhere to visit, a place of pilgrimage in some new, modern sense of the word, now that cars and tour buses could provide the transport. Yet that seemed so much at odds with what I had heard of Fatima with its thousands of pilgrims, often on foot, travelling great distances to the shrine for the thirteenth of each month.

I left Bom Jesus in awe of the magnificence of the concept but feeling no empathy with its manifestation, no connection with the throng, like a man turning away from a church because he felt no community of spirit with its followers.

I looked at the map and walked on, wondering why my spirits were so low.

Shortly afterwards I entered the Noise Zone. The countryside was pleasant to travel through. There were hills and forests and little villages peeping out from behind them but here the sweet music of silence was entirely absent. Nearby I could hear the dull whine of a chain saw. In the distance there was the staccato rattle of motorbikes and the shrill, insistent scream of car horns blaring, at what I knew not.

There was no big town nearby to make a ready explanation. Then I heard the dogs barking, yapping, yelping, one with the loudest, most persistent, most continuous bark I have ever heard. It was miles away but it pierced the air like the waves of white noise used as a torture by evil regimes.

The fish man kept his hand on the horn as his van screeched across the hills and valleys, until he passed me on this narrow, leafy, rural road, empty of habitations or people, except for the two of us.

A few miles later I rounded a corner and a rowdy group of children were waiting for the school bus. The revolution of 1974 brought schooling to all but there were not enough schools, necessitating in some areas, that children attend in half day shifts. It was 12 noon so this must have been the second shift.

They roared and yelled at each other, fighting and shouting like demented hyenas. They took no notice of the stranger and I walked through the throng as if I were invisible to them. An hour later I reached the school and, although the bus had arrived and safely delivered the second shift, work had not yet begun. The same crowd were in the playground, racing around, screaming, pulling and hauling at each other. The noise was phenomenal, I swear it made the wooden school building shake.

I had left Bom Jesus in low spirits. Before I reached the Noise Zone I had cheered up a little but once in it I felt as if I had been directed here to endure a penance, for what I knew not. I quickened the pace and sped on as fast as tiring legs would allow, racing away from this rackety part of the countryside

The first good omen was the solid stone walls of the buildings of a village. Once within them the noise ended as if they had been built to keep it out.

Four women were on their way to the fields, without hurry and in their own good time, laden with implements and provisions. Two carried long-handled sythes, short-bladed but much longer in the handle than I had ever seen before. They were all dressed in unrelieved black, black dresses, black stockings and shoes, black head scarves.

The oldest was like a ball of country butter, round and cheerful, droplets of moisture glistening on her face. She had a sythe over one shoulder and a wicker basket of food and wine hooked in the crook of the other arm. Her hair was pulled back from her face. Her head covering hung down her back almost to her waist and she made it swish from side to side as she spoke. Her shoes were the lightest of black pumps and, like some large women seem able to do in spite of their bulk, she stepped as lightly and nimbly as a tiny Olympic gymnast.

I greeted them in Portuguese and the butter ball engaged me in merry chat. The other three spoke civilly enough but looked at her as if unable to understand why she was in such good form when they were on the way to a long afternoon's work in the fields.

The butter ball said something to me very loudly and distinctly. Without being sure of what she was saying I knew by her tone and her glad eye that it was by way of an invitation. I thought she was asking me to join them at their work in the fields, with the promise of sharing the food and wine if I tried hard. I shrugged.

'Obrigado.' I said. 'Estou com pressa.' I would have wished to put it more courteously but 'Thank you. I'm in a hurry.' was the best I could manage.

They all roared with laughter and I knew then that the invitation was not just to share the work in the fields. I smiled and laughed with them, wishing I had the words in their language to join in the banter.

The butter ball pulled the cork of a bottle of wine and reached it to me. It was a light shade of red and the barrel of the bottle flashed like a ruby in the sunlight. I took a swig and it was cool, almost cold, fresh and tangy, tasting of wild blackberries. She knew that I liked it.

'Mais vinho?' she said and this time I knew what she meant.

I took another long draught and handed the bottle back to her with a grin. She wiped the neck with the back of her hand, took a sip herself and put the cork back.

We walked on in opposite directions and every few step they turned to roar back at me. I had no idea what they were calling. Was it shouts of encouragement, flattery, ribald temptations, jokes at my expense? Whatever it was, it was certainly without malice. It was a little fun amongst friends.

This encounter had soothed the aches of the Noise Zone. The women and I had cheered each other on our separate ways. They sounded in great good humour and now they had something to talk about all afternoon. It was a second good omen. For me the gloom had gone. They had made my day.

My route lay amongst the wooded hills and I came to a gap in the forest on the left hand side. Half a mile away there were people working in the fields. As I watched, an animal slipped out of the forest to my right. It was bigger than a large dog, loping easily with stiff legged strides. Its head was turned away from me towards the people in the fields for, although they were much further away, they were upwind and I was downwind.

I had seen that shaggy coat and effortless lope before but never from such close range. In the Elburz Mountains of Iran, I sat on a rocky ridge and watched in awe as wolves ran the track on the other side of a steep valley. I had seen their tracks in the mountains of Turkey and Afghanistan, one set of paw prints measuring almost 4" across.

In those countries the shepherds still use big dogs to protect the sheep, as well as smaller ones to keep the flock together. In Ireland the wolf is long gone but the huge Irish wolfhound, a veritable giant of a dog and a most unlikely looking pet, remains as a symbol of man's fear of the wolf.

On my previous walk in Spain I had met shepherds with huge guard dogs but had been sceptical when I was told by a fellow pilgrim to beware of the wolves in the mountains of Monte Irago. At the time I had thought the wolf extinct in Spain. Later I was to learn that, although this magnificent beast is now rare even in the wildest recesses of Europe, there is still a sizable population in Romania, perhaps 2,000. A recent survey has shown too that there are between 1,500 and 2,000 wolves still at large in Spain and Portugal, most of these in the north-west of the peninsula. They feed now on farm rubbish and scavenge village refuse dumps but, amongst the villagers, the primaeval fear of the wolf is as strong as ever.

I paused on the verge and watched. The people in the fields saw nothing but this great animal held them in its gaze as it crossed the road and skirted the forest on the far side. The wooded peaks were close and it would be amongst them in a few minutes.

My fortunes had changed and I knew that this third good omen predicted a fascinating end to what had started as a disquieting day.

I saw it first perched on top on the highest of the hills. The ruins of an ancient village standing sentinel above the rugged terrain. The little road, winding its way to the city of Guimarães, skirted the hill, climbing steeply and, at the crest, I entered Citânia de Briteiros, once the Celtic stronghold from which this countryside was ruled.

All around me were the remnants of an intriguing past, stone buildings, some circular, others square or rectangular in ground plan. Although I was born and have lived my life in a Celtic country, this was the first time I had seen the shape and thus could imagine the substance of a village built by the Celts 2000 years ago.

It had been constructed to a plan which fitted it to the slopes at the top of the hill, but it was the round houses which gave this place its special character. Two had been rebuilt and were as strongly made as ancient Irish round towers, their conical roofs thatched and firmly secured.

There were water pipes which once fed fountains and a building with carved lintels now considered to have been a bath house.

There were walls and paved streets at different levels between the ruins of the houses, like the narrow streets of more modern villages I had passed through in the past few days. In Ireland the paved area between the farm house or the cottage and the out-buildings is also known as 'the street' and the likeness was uncanny, similar stones and the same skills in working them.

There are perhaps 40 of these villages in Northern Portugal. Some date to the 5th or 6th centuries BC, others are much earlier. The story is that this one, Citânia de Briteiros, was the last Celtic stronghold to fall to the Romans in the 1st century BC. So impressed were the conquerors at the valour of its defenders that, once the victory had been won, the Roman Consul handed back the control of the village to the inhabitants.

The view is of hundreds of miles of countryside, across clumps of wooded hills split by steep valleys, to the big peaks to the north and east, holding the border with Spain.

A Roman writer of the 1st century described the life of these Celts as living simply, having water and beer to drink and sleeping on the ground. For most of the year their main food was bread made from roasted, ground acorns.

The little wine they had was saved for celebrations and when they gathered to eat and drink, they sat in a row by rank. Their music was made on the flute and horn. Their dances involved leaping high in the air and landing in a crouch, like Cossack dancers. The modern Celt would have felt as much at home amongst such festivities as he or she would at an Irish ceilidhe.

I sat inside a tiny, round ruin of a house at the very summit of the hill and gave myself time to feel this place. If there were any other visitors on the site they were neither to be seen nor heard. The broken walls were shoulder height as I sat, as if arranged to let me see Portugal from this perch. The stone at my back was warm and firm, my seat the yielding turf. I stretched my legs full length and the tiredness of the past seven days sat more easily on me than I had a right to expect.

Citânia de Briteiros

Once again I had reached a place which seemed strangely familiar, not the familiarity which might imply that I had been here before. It was more a sense of being at ease here, of being comfortable amongst these stones which once were homes.

My father had been born in the county of Devon in England and had come to live in Ireland as a young man. On one occasion, when I was a teenager, I had countered a remark of his about Ireland by doubting what he would know about the subject, he being only a Englishman. It was an arrogant response, only mitigated by my youth and the fact that it was said without malice. He was irritated, not so much by my rudeness but the remark.

'I'm not an Englishman.' he said with a rare flash of annoyance. 'I'm a Devon man.'

It was the end of the discussion and, without being able to explain the statement, even to myself, I felt I knew what he meant. Young as I was, I was aware that there was more communication between us than was ever expressed in words.

I went back to his birthplace near North Molton in Devon a year ago and found that a family tree traced the line back to a Norman family of the 15th century. Earlier my son had discovered that the name Slader meant 'the man of the forest glade', 'slade' being the old Norman word for a forest glade. The riddle of my father's remark seemed solved. Had he meant that his forbears were Normans not Anglo-Saxons?

Later I learned that descendants of the Celtic Bretons who had been driven from the south-west of England by the Anglo-Saxons 500 years earlier had returned with William the Conqueror in the 11th century. So impressed was William by the support of the Celtic Bretons, they were rewarded with gifts of land, particularly in south-west England where Gaelic had remained the common language. The Celts had returned.

Had my father meant that he too was a Norman Celt? The family build was certainly Celtic. And could such a folk memory explain my feeling of ease and comfort in this place? Had I travelled back to the roots of my race?

I neither knew nor cared how long I sat. The Demon of Urgency had fled. On such a journey tourist time-tables and the need to see just one more wonder before the day's end, make no sense at all. The spirit must be ready to move.

When I felt it was time to go I heard an excited cry, then another. A school party had arrived to see the site and were swarming up the hill to the summit. But this was no screaming mob like the second school-shift earlier in the day.

They, like me, were would-be travellers in the past. I knew that the teacher would make sure they had all the historical facts. But I hoped that there might be a chance for them to sit down in silence for a few moments and feel the place as I had done. Would any of them have that feeling of touching the past which had been my experience of Citânia de Briteiros?

I hoped that, if not now, sometime in their lives they might be so fortunate.

The road to Guimarães was so peaceful, almost entirely devoid of traffic but I remember nothing of the countryside. My mind was back in Citânia de Briteiros while my legs took my body onwards to the resting place for the night. When I reached the outskirts I knew I had taken the long way between the two cities but it had been a day in a lifetime.

The unreasoned lowness of spirit after Bom Jesus had been followed by the clamour of the Noise Zone. The wolf flitting across the countryside had broken the spell of melancholy and the butter ball and her friends had raised the day. Then the Celtic village on the hill had crowned it with an experience like a mystical revelation.

I was not in the least surprised to find the city of Guimarães as accessible, congenial and historically captivating as Braga. It was an ideal place to rest and recuperate with a glass of cool white port in the evening sunshine.

I ate when the sun went down in a tiny, traditional restaurant. The speciality of the house was caldeirada, served in a large earthenware crock, too delicious a dish to be described merely as fish stew.

The Vinho Verde accompanied it perfectly. Vinho Verde, literally green wine, so-called, not for its colour, but because it is young, can be white or golden or even red. It is the wine of the Minho Region and is fresh and light, with a very distinctive flavour.

The wine is made from grapes which, as they mature, are not too sweet because they have been allowed to ripen slowly on vines that are trained across high supports. They are less affected by the reflected heat from the ground and the result is a wine of low alcohol strength, often only 8°, but full of flavour. I had been enjoying it with my food each evening since I crossed into Portugal.

I went elsewhere for dessert, two pastries which would have been a credit to a French patisserie and, when the evening was at an end, strolled back to the inn and slept the sleep of the content.

CHAPTER 7

Across the River of Gold

In the cool, damp air of the early morning I walked away from Guimarães feeling more refreshed and rested than I would have expected after the last four strenuous days on the go. My route was on quiet country roads but, as before, my mind was still in the place I had left behind.

Guimarães had been so accessible historically that its claim to be the cradle of Portugal's nationhood, which had seemed far too grandiose before, now appeared obvious. It is so called because it is the birthplace, in the 12th century, of the founder of the Kingdom of Portugal, Dom Alfonso Henriques.

His father, Henry of Burgundy, built the impressive Castelo whose great square keep and castellated towers overlook the city. It stands like a monument to the Reconquest of the country from the Moors and the establishment of the kingdom.

I had been taken too, by the Art-Deco appearances of some of the shops and cafés. One patisserie shop would not have been out of place on a smart boulevard in Paris in the nineteen twenties. After dinner, I had let the evening pass at its own speed, resting easily in a café with a stunning set of six mirrors which would have graced an art gallery devoted to the period.

Thinking about Guimarães shortened the walk on these pleasant country side-roads and the damp day turned to rain.

I came out on the main road near a village where the carriage way was cambered around a steep bend. A minibus, travelling towards Porto met the curve too fast. It spun in a circle in front of me, slewing across the full width of the road. The minibus seemed to rotate slowly, tracing an almost elegant shape on the tarmac. The centrifugal force of the spin and the disorientation effect, as the world revolved around them, must have been terrifying to the occupants.

I could see the fear in the face of the driver as he slid past me. His passengers were all young and their faces white as they spun close to me in their turn. No doubt there had been great fun on board as they hurtled towards Porto, but in one brief pause between comedy and tragedy, their very lives were in the toss of fate's coin. Heads they live, tails they die.

The minibus scrunched on to the gravel of the verge and stopped. The driver laid his face on the steering wheel and linked his hands across the top of his head. Had he collapsed in relief? Was it a prayer of thanks for deliverance?

They were coming from the right direction to have been on a visit to Bom Jesus. If that was so, had they climbed the steps or taken the minibus to the top?

If I had been in any doubt about whether I should walk on to Porto along this road or take the bus, my mind was made up for me. The past four days had been long routes and five hours walking on this day seemed far enough. In the village I had a coffee and decided to wait for the bus.

Near the time, the owner of the café sent his sixteen-year-old son with me to make sure I caught the right bus. We were not able to converse but he grinned at me reassuringly, confident my transport would arrive. From time to time his father came to the door of the café to make sure the boy had not deserted his post. This simple gesture of concern for the traveller personified the true spirit of the human kindness of the Portuguese. No reward was expected nor indeed would one have been welcomed.

In a world where increasing affluence seems to preempt the possibility of courtesy, this small kindness demonstrated that thoughtfulness for the stranger still exists in Europe. I was moved.

I left the bus on the outskirts to walk into Porto, the second city of Portugal. The situation is magnificent, on a steep site perched above a gorge at the mouth of the great Rio Douro, the River of Gold.

The citizens are quietly proud of a traditional saying . . .

'Coimbra sings: Braga prays: Lisbon shows off: Porto works.'

It is a prosperous place, industrious, busy, business-like. There are affluent suburbs and a sprawl of commercial building and dwellings but it was the compact heart of the city which drew me to it. There its treasures are hidden as if the inhabitants feel no need to show them off.

I found a comfortable room in a small pensão near the centre. Later I learned that it was meant to be in the middle of the red light district but, if there was such a trade nearby it was plied so discreetly, I was unaware of it until I was returning to my room at the end of the evening.

I was due, maybe even overdue, a rest day and Patricia and Norman, friends of my friends in Cascais, entertained me to a wonderful meal at a quay-side restaurant and arranged an introduction to the head of one of the most famous firms in the Port wine trade.

Patricia and Norman are in the clothing business and had come to

Porto to manufacture clothes for the fashion market because of the hard-working reputation of the people.

They had to contact my pensão on a number of occasions to arrange to meet me and were impressed to find that not only was I an esteemed guest whose arrangements were of urgent concern but the senhora in charge was attending to my interests like she would a favourite relation come to stay. Patricia told me they had never been so well treated when they stayed in the top hotels.

But it was no surprise to me. The senhora and her relations running the pensão spoke no English and my words of Portuguese were few and inadequate but they were according me the same civility, helpfulness and kindness that I come to accept as normal in Portugal. Not only were they glad to see me as a customer, I was truly an honoured guest.

In Porto the contrasts in social life were woven into the very fabric of the city. There were fine modern buildings beside a gipsy encampment on a derelict site. Young children and stray dogs were rooting through the rubbish bins outside expensive restaurants. There were beggars on the streets and beautifully dressed women strolling, window shopping, taking life at the pace of the leisured.

But there was no sense of hidden menace, no feeling that behind the busy facade of daily living the have-nots were so affronted and frustrated by the obvious inequalities, that rage might cause an eruption of theft or violence. Many modern cities, for all their evidence of progress, seem vulnerable to such crime. It lurks in the shadows, unseen but not unsensed. Its pattern appears unreasoned only because its manifestation is often drug-related.

Portugal is not immune to this type of crime but it appears to be confined to the popular resort areas where the display of the opulence of the rich is at its most obvious.

I saw the cathedral on a rise in front of me and wandered towards it. An elderly lady reached the door before me and found the catch too stiff. I helped her make it work and she thanked me with gentle dignity and an old-world courtesy which now we find hard to match.

Perhaps it set the feeling of my visit, for I found the cathedral a most peaceful and comfortable place to be.

In the 12th century it was constructed as a fortified church and added to over the years. It has a Romanesque rose window like one I had seen at Portomarin in Spain on my previous walk. There is a Baroque doorway and the cloisters are 14th century Gothic decorated later with azulejos, the tiled murals which are such a splendid feature of Portuguese art.

I sat for a long time in a pew half-way back. I heard the people come and go, but only faintly, as if they were trying not to disturb me. They prayed, the words lost in a mantra drone. They read the guide book to each other, mentally ticking off the features of this great edifice. High heels clattered across uncarpeted sections of the floor.

I wondered what I was doing here, in no hurry at all, finding it easy to meditate.

This journey had, so far, felt very different from the Road to Santiago two years before. Then the almost overwhelming loneliness of the first few days had been replaced by an acute sense of purpose and a mystical feeling for the pilgrimage which, although I knew I did not understand the logic of it, had become one of the most exciting inspirations of my life.

Now the mystical dimension was being shown to me in glimpses only and I was a little disappointed – on reflection, probably unreasonably so, for I had been only ten days on the road and such rewards require patience. They will arrive, if at all, in their own good time.

At that moment I decided to change my route. Instead of heading inland immediately after Porto, I would keep to the coast for 100 kilometres or so and then strike inland again for the very heart of Portugal.

With this decision now made, I left the cathedral feeling much more cheerful than I had done for days. On starting the journey I had not set a specific finishing point. I knew now that this had not given me a greater freedom to wander, and in some vague way it had been undermining my sense of purpose.

It seemed obvious now that I should try to reach the south coast at the point where the Portuguese Algarve meets the Spanish border on the Gulf of Cadiz. The Rio Guadiana forms the frontier between the two countries and I could end my journey by crossing the last of the rivers of Portugal to finish in Spain.

The effect of this declaration of intent was so strong that it seemed to lift the tiredness from me like a burden from my back. Far from feeling like a restriction on my wanderings, it gave me a feeling of freedom, as if all this journey had lacked was a destination.

That evening I celebrated this new sense of purpose in the dining annex of a little bar. I had heard that the citizens of Porto are proud to be called 'tripeiros', the tripe eaters. The story is that when Henry the Navigator was equipping to attack the Moors at Ceuta, he took all the cattle from the region to victual his fleet, leaving only the offal. The locals, quite properly, made a virtue out of necessity and the nickname, 'tripeiros', stuck. Tripe is still a favourite dish in Porto and, served in the local style, is a delicious stew with beans.

I had thus no choice to make. It had to be tripe for my little celebration. Portuguese restaurants usually offer main dishes in full or half portions and there is no pressure to take the full portion when a half will do. No doubt the half is very suitable in the middle of the day or to satisfy a small appetite or for those with an uneasy conscience about eating too much. I had no such inhibitions and my tripe arrived as a great steaming dish, tender, succulent, a proper meal for a travelling man.

I remembered with mouth-watering pleasure my mother serving tripe with onions and white sauce for the evening meal we called tea, when I came home from school. There was no shortage of tripe during World War 2 or immediately after it, when rationing was at its most severe. My mother used to say it was only plentiful because most people did not know how to cook it.

I remembered that the tripe needed hours of cooking to ensure it was tender. She hated the smell in the house when it was boiling but the dish was worth it. The onions could be added later in big chunks and would be firm and crunchy, just the way my father and I liked them.

Tripe in the Porto style was a very different dish but, like my mother's tripe and onions in the Ulster style, it was the classic combination of good ingredients, perfectly cooked, appetising, sustaining, delicious.

Thus far on the trip I had been drinking Vinho Verde with my evening meal but on this evening I had the red wine from the Douro Valley. It was straight from the barrel, served by the tumbler and its price included. I guessed that it would be stronger than the Vinho Verde so, much as I was enjoying it with the meal, I made sure not to pass my tumbler to the barman too often for a refill. I needed to be fresh for the morrow.

Porto in the late evening was a most pleasant experience. Its old streets were crowded with lively, friendly people patronising the bars and cafés, strolling with their friends. For me, the stranger on his own, and without speaking to anyone, there was no feeling of being alone amongst the crowd. I had only been here a few hours but my acquaintance with Porto seemed longer. I was born and brought up in a city but have never since wanted to live in one. However, a visit is a different matter and this was my kind of place.

Next morning, and with the luxury of a whole rest day in front of me, I wandered through the steep streets and alleyways of the old town.

Porto's hidden secrets revealed themselves to me as I explored its streets, the great glass domed market, startling views of the river and its dramatic bridges spanning the gorge, the Clérigos tower, said to be the tallest structure in the country. The ugliness of industry and commerce which all cities share was pushed into the background. Here, there was great tradition and antiquity, I was finding it a fascinating, exciting and – almost unbelievable for such a big city – even a charming place to be.

In the early afternoon I crossed the Rio Douro by the double-decker Luis 1st road bridge and was glad to be on foot. I could stop and stare from the height of its span. It was the most spectacular view of the river and its city.

Across the bridge lies Vila Nova de Gaia, a suburb, but more like a small town in its own right, looking Porto in the eye from its perch on the other side of the river.

This is the heart and centre of the port trade. From the bridge I looked down on the red-tiled roofs of the wine lodges, their famous names whitewashed in giant letters, Sandyman, Graham, Taylor, Cockburn.

There are some eighty of these lodges, to which the wines made in the vineyards of the upper stretches of the Douro are brought to be blended and matured.

Moored along the waterfront were the beautiful traditional boats, the barcos rabelos, once used to carry the wine barrels down river from the vineyards to the wine lodges. Then stretches of the river were narrow and so fast flowing that only these small boats could make the journey. Now they lie off their companies' wharves advertising the great names on colourful sails in grand and dignified fashion.

I strolled on across the bridge and searched the maze of alleyways in Vila Nova de Gaia for the lodge of my appointment with the wine trade. I was due to meet Michael Symington of the family which controls the largest of the port wine companies still privately owned and to make my weekly broadcast on Radio Ulster from his office.

A charming member of his staff helped me make contact with the BBC in Belfast, in spite of the fact that the direct line to the studio was down. Last time, the phone had been on a bar counter, with the roar of the election outside and the electronic music of the fruit machine at my elbow. This time, I had the calm and quiet of a comfortable office, as I told the listeners tales of crossing the mountains to Gerês, of Bom Jesus and the Celtic village of Briteiros.

Later Michael Symington talked to me about port with the passion of a man who sees his life's work as a gift from the gods. His company's labels include Dow, Graham and Warr and his family have been in the business for 150 years, relative newcomers, as he said with a deprecating smile.

He explained that other famous wines like Burgundy, Claret, Sherry and Champagne had been exceedingly highly regarded in their local areas before they became popular elsewhere, but Port had been developed in a very different way.

Over three hundred years ago the wars between Britain and France were having a serious effect on trade. British merchants began scouring the friendlier parts of Europe for a source of wine to replace the Claret imported from Bordeaux. They discovered that there was a suitable wine being made in large quantities in the Upper Douro Valley and began to ship it home.

The first consignment arrived in an undrinkable state because the rough crossing of the Bay of Biscay had caused fermentation to begin again. They managed to sell the wine by adding brandy, but for the next shipment the spirit was added to the wine before it left Porto. Thus one of the most important wine trades in the world was established.

Now the brandy is added before the fermentation process has been completed and the resulting wine takes its sweetness only from its grapes. Vintage Port, which matures in the bottle, is, of course, the top of the range and the most expensive. Tawny and Ruby Port are matured in great casks for at least three years and form the bulk of the market.

White Port is not as readily available in Britain or Ireland but, served chilled, it is a favourite aperitif in Portugal. Its dry version is between Fino and Amontillado Sherry and I had already discovered its refreshing qualities between the end of a day's walk and the evening meal.

Michael explained, with great patience, the workings of the trade and showed me around the processes of blending and maturing in the lodge. For such a carefully regulated and business-like operation there was an obviously civilised approach and a sense of style, which must have been important factors in the development of the Port trade over the past 350 years.

I was learning 'mouth to ear'. A few years before I had heard Michael Volin, one of the greatest teachers of yoga in the world, say that this was how he had learned from the sages of the East.

As I returned across the bridge, mind still full of the world of Michael Symington and a bottle of his best tucked under my arm, a friendly voice greeted me.

'Hey, travelling man. We meet again!'

It was two of the four New Zealanders I had spoken to in Gerês. They were on their way to visit the wine lodges, hoping to join a tasting of the product. One of them produced a Portuguese/English phrase book from his pocket.

'Its down to you, sport.' he said grinning, 'You told us we should go to Porto to buy a phrase book and to enjoy a city and not to miss the local brew.'

It was good to see them again, but not a surprise. They had come a long way to Europe, but were now on a very different journey. They would be travelling men themselves before they knew it.

That evening Patricia and Norman invited me to a meal in a wonderful dockside restaurant where they were entertaining a buying delegation from a German fashion house.

The trend setters from the fashion house were late, of course, they had so many little things to take seriously while they were in this part of the world. It left me with the great advantage of having time to talk to Patricia and Norman.

In modern life conversation is often squeezed for room and on my walk the occasions when a common language made it possible had been few and very far between. This was a chance to talk to two perceptive and concerned people, who had lived and worked here for years.

In ways, my short time in the country had been different from what they would have expected and they were as interested in my experiences as I was by theirs. Patricia felt that my way of travelling, my few possessions on my back, staying in the simplest of accommodation, had been of great advantage in making contact with the people quickly and naturally.

The fashion experts arrived and we were treated to a glorious meal. To start, we had lagostim, which is a huge prawn, as big as a small lobster and was the house speciality. Then I had cabrito or young goat. The cabrito, once translated, caused a wrinkling of noses amongst some of the fashion house guests but when they saw this delicious dish served, they ordered it too.

I slept well in my comfortable room, in the friendly pension, in this fascinating city. Next day I was away early, well rested and refreshed, with my bottle of Michael's best still un-opened in my rucksac.

I left Porto in the most spectacular way, over the Luis 1st Bridge, across the River of Gold, my third great river of Portugal.

CHAPTER 8

The Tale of the Lost Sole

Vila Nova de Gaia seemed much bigger once I was amongst its streets, trying to find a route along the coast to Espinho. To be sure I was going the right way I asked a young man for directions. He surprised me by answering in English and politely enquired if he might walk with me to show me the way and practise speaking English.

He was in his early twenties, smartly dressed, slightly formal in manner. It was obviously intriguing to him to find a foreigner walking around his country by choice. I asked him what he did for a living.

'I am a car designer.' He said with a little smile. 'If everyone travelled like you I would be soon out of work.' We laughed together and I encouraged him to talk on. He talked about his work and living in Porto. Now he had the chance to speak to an interested stranger he intended to make the most of it.

'It is hard for me to say, but there are too many cars in our cities.' He looked at me, seriously, as if hoping that this heresy against the cult of the car would not offend me. 'Soon we will have to plan for cities without cars.'

It was easy to take his point, most cities I have visited are near or beyond crisis point. The great invention for the convenient transport of the masses is clogging highways as fast as they can be built.

We reached a cross-roads where our ways parted and he shook hands with me, touchingly grateful, as if I had been the one with something important to say. There are times when an interested listener is more appreciated than an interesting speaker.

My pleasant side road joined a main road without a verge and the walking became a survival course. I searched for a lane or a path nearer the sea but there was none. It was a relief to stop in mid-morning for a coffee in a way-side bar. The big TV screen featured Paul Simon singing in English about a girl who had diamonds on the soles of her shoes.

My mind flashed an image, brighter than the TV screen. I could see her travelling, flying without wings, her feet never touching the ground. It was impressive to a mere pedestrian like me but I was not in the least envious. There would be a price and she would have no choice but pay it.

At the end of the afternoon, with nearly twenty miles behind me, I reached a village near the sea and found all the accommodation was closed. It was too early in the season, they told me, although by now, it was the second week in June.

As usual there was someone to help. A man arranged a lift in a works' mini-bus back to the resort of Espinho and there I stayed in comfort in a small hotel. Next morning I took a train back to where I had finished the previous afternoon and walked on.

I was still on a road but this one was quiet, close to the sea, reaching south along a narrow, sandy finger of land between the bay of Aveiro and the Atlantic Ocean. The villages were fascinating, the road linking them through little forests, between the sand hills to the fishing port of São Jacinto at the southerly tip of the peninsula. It was still 20 miles away but I felt sure I would find an inn open at the end of another long day.

The dullness of the morning cleared and the day became hot well before my lunch break. There had been warm walking on some of the previous days, but this was real heat.

Two days before, the sole of one of my fine walking shoes had begun to show the wear and tear of the journey. They were meant to be good shoes, well-made as far as I could tell. They were the product of a famous firm of mountain boot manufacturers and because of that, not cheap and the only footwear I had with me.

The one piece sole of the right shoe had begun to part from the upper at the heel. The first sign had been as I walked towards Porto but on this day it decided to part a little further. Perhaps it was the heat or my spring-heeled stride or simply glue fatigue. The miles passed pleasantly except for the slap of sole on upper as the foot swung forward. Soon it was more than half way off and flapping like a seal's flipper.

I smiled to myself, a little grimly I must admit, but the flapping sole, serious though it might be, was less of a problem than the blisters I had suffered at the beginning of the walk to Santiago. Soon, I reasoned, I would be in São Jacinto where there would be a boot mender's and a comfortable inn for the night.

It may have looked close on the map but getting there in the heat of the hottest part of the afternoon, having to consciously lift my right foot and place it on the ground again, one step further, without totally dislodging the sole, required serious concentration.

I cheered myself with an image from my first mountaineering expedition, to the Taurus Mountains in Eastern Turkey. One of my companions was Victor Bateman, a senior civil servant and enthusiastic bird watcher – the ornithologist amongst the mountaineers – the birdman amongst the rock apes – as another old friend put it.

Victor had refused to wear mountaineering boots on principle, never having taken to the idea of such uncomfortable footwear. All members of the expedition were meant to have boots, so Victor deliberately ordered the wrong size shortly before we left, so that he would not have to take the boots with him.

Once there, his trusty walking shoes were soon cut to pieces on the sharp rocks of the Turkish mountains and Victor had to borrow a pair of black gym shoes, size 13. The miracle was that any of the others had feet so big.

In my mind's eye I could see the tall, stooped figure, sketch book in one hand, pencil poised in the other, focussing on some unsuspecting bird in the middle distance, as he hopped amongst the rocks towards it like a great black crow.

Remembering Victor gave me a surge of strength from past friendship. Seven years after the Turkish expedition, the year he was 66, he went with me to Afghanistan, this time to take charge of the base camp with the expedition doctor. His spirit and cheerfulness were legendary and when he died of cancer, six months later, his wife told me that his last year had been the most fulfilling of his life.

Like Victor, I had no second pair of shoes. I needed to have mine mended. In São Jacinto I asked in a café on the sea front for the whereabouts of 'o sapaterio', the shoe mender. The owner looked at my shoe and shook his head. There was no sapaterio in the village.

Down a side street I found a bar full of fishermen. I tried again and this time there was concern as well as sympathy. Soon ten or twelve men were gathered around me. Even the card game stopped for a few moments.

The debate about what should be done, took time and, at one stage was quite heated. I was left in the background and one of the men fetched a piece of cardboard so that I could stand on it in my stocking foot. The barman, large and friendly, avoided the debate and concentrated on the practicalities. He produced a bar stool which had been carefully concealed on his side of the counter and placed a large cool beer in front of me.

Suddenly the argument was over and four men emerged as the victors. One was in his sixties, his skin nearly as dark and wrinkled as his brown corduroy jerkin. Another, in a blue wind jacket, was the same age and a third was younger, dressed in denim overalls. The fourth was probably the oldest, with grizzled grey hair and a grey sweater the same shade as my own on top of his working shirt. He appointed himself my special protector and cleared the others back so that I had plenty of space at the bar.

Blue wind jacket was chosen to be in charge. Brown corduroy jerkin was sent for the materials and he fetched contact adhesive, a large file and a scraper. Denim overalls was allowed to prepare the surfaces of the sole and the upper with the scraper and file while the others took turns at reading the instructions on the adhesive packet.

When he was ready, blue wind jacket called the company to order and applied the glue to both surfaces. I gathered that the glue had to be left for ten minutes. While we waited, my protector explained that, although there was a good place to eat in São Jacinto, there was no where to stay for the night. He spoke so slowly and carefully that I found I could understand him quite well. I gathered that when the shoe was mended he would see me on my way to somewhere to stay.

My new friend told me that he had been a fisherman, but an accident at sea had left him with the stiff leg and meant he had to retire. He was interested in my journey and I used the map to show my route. When he told the others about my travels through Portugal, there were nods of understanding. They approved.

When the ten minutes were up, the whole company watched as blue wind jacket joined the two surfaces together with a theatrical flourish. All he needed was something to keep the pressure of upper on sole for a few moments. Someone suggested that he should put the shoe under the leg of a chair.

The nearest chair belonged to one of the card players, with a gaudy picture of a sailing ship on the back of his plastic jacket. He was asked to get up and let the shoe under a leg of his chair. He must have been on a losing streak.

'He's French.' he yelled angrily and kicked his chair over, as if to be French was some special crime which needed no explanation here.

The bar erupted with indignation and the card player was surrounded by shouting, pushing men. As he was thrown out on to the street, I looked at the barman and he was standing, resting his weight on the counter on his huge hands. He smiled as if the retribution was just.

When the shoe was ready, I put it on with some ceremony and bought a round of drinks for everyone in the bar. The card player appeared in the doorway to apologise and they let him in on my request.

I left the bar to shouts of good wishes and my protector wheeled his bicycle as we walked slowly to the quayside. When we reached the ferry, my friend had a long chat with the captain. They were obviously talking about me. The captain was a burly, unsmiling, dark-haired man. He raised his peaked cap and wiped his brow. He glowered in my direction and nodded me on board as the crew prepared to cast off.

As I shook hands with my protector and friend I knew that we were parting sadly, as if we were aware of the unlikelihood that we would ever meet again. With no more than a few words in common, I was sure we understood each other, that this retired fishermen and I knew each other, perhaps better than many friends of long standing.

The ferry was a proper boat, made for rough crossings and would have held perhaps forty or fifty passengers. There were about fifteen of us when she put to sea and, when the fares were being collected, the seaman with the tickets would take no money from me. By way of explanation he pointed at the broad back of the captain.

It was a most enjoyable passage, first gliding along in the calm of the bay, then pushing through choppy waves, as we crossed the narrow mouth where Atlantic rollers met the solid mass of water stored behind the great spit of sand.

We disembarked at a little jetty and, from the map, I could see we were near the town of Praia da Barra. I sat on a wall, trying to get my bearings and realised that the captain was towering over me. For such a big man he was light on his feet and had approached me as quietly as an assassin.

Without the faintest smile of helpfulness he motioned me to stay where I was, indicating with gestures, that I was not to move away from this spot. It was confusing but I appeared to have no choice other than obey orders.

Ten minutes later a bus arrived and the captain came back to lead me to it. He talked at length to the driver and shook hands with me with the force of a boat grinding against a jetty wall. He smiled for the first time as we said good-bye.

The bus driver repulsed my attempts to pay. Unlike the ferry captain who obviously felt that any attempt to talk to me in Portuguese would be a waste of time, he chatted easily to me, not bothered in the least at the lack of coherent reply.

By what seemed to me to be an almost circular route, he delivered me to a café, passed on the message to the only customer and instructed him to keep an eye on me. I was bemused by what was happening, uncertain of what was expected of me, perplexed even, so I ordered a coffee and a couple of sugary doughnuts and stayed cool. When the customer had to leave, he passed his duties on to the barman.

Another bus arrived and the barman shepherded me towards it. Once again there was a conversation with the driver and no doubt that I was the subject of their discussions.

The driver waved away my feeble attempt to pay as if it was totally irrelevant and this time we appeared to be going somewhere. My bewilderment began to ease as we arrived in the main street of a seaside town in the early evening.

On one side of the road there were well kept gardens. On the other the houses were two-storeyd wooden structures, well-made and proudly cared for. They were freshly painted in white with broad vertical stripes of red, green or blue, resplendently showy in their summer holiday colours.

This was Costa Nova and, although there were very few people about and certainly not many visitors, it had a most cheerful, charming air. It was as if this place was permanently on vacation.

The driver stopped the bus opposite an inn, the Pensão/Restaurante Fernando, and pointed.

'Bom pensão, bom restaurante, baratto.' He spoke slowly and distinctly, saying one word at a time, and with a little knowing nod of the head. 'Good inn, good restaurant, cheap.'

Now that I had arrived all was revealed. The retired fisherman, who had become my guide and protector in São Jacinto, had set the process in motion by transferring me into the care of the captain of the ferry. The message had been relayed and the care of the stranger had been passed along this chain of friendship. Now I was safely delivered to a place where I could find a bed and a meal.

I was impressed and moved to realise that one chance contact had led to such kindness from these men, each of whom owed it to his predecessor to fulfil an act of caring for someone they did not know.

The inn evoked the atmosphere of the past. My room was reached along a veranda and was small and cosy, like my bedroom in a wooden seaside bungalow my mother once rented for the summer, on the coast of County Down, when I was a teenager.

On first going to my room, I had to pass a landing on the metal fire escape. Chained there was a boxer dog, large and fierce, snarling and snapping at me but held by his chain so that I had room to pass. On leaving the room later, his anger had gone. He was welcoming and friendly, accepting me without as much as a bark, knowing now that I was a guest not an intruder.

During the time I was there, I never saw him released from his chain. He did his dropping over the edge of the metal landing and they fell on waste ground below. We became friends, as if he knew I meant him well. He roused himself from bored torpor and cheered up when he heard me coming. I always stopped to pass the time of day with him, or night, because the lavatory was just beyond his prison. He minded not in the least being wakened from his sleep when I answered a call of nature in the dark hours. It gave us another opportunity for a chat.

But every time I passed I felt sorry for his lot. This beautiful animal, his loyalty taken for granted, without the human or canine contact he would have appreciated, so grateful for a kind word, even in a language he was not supposed to understand.

William Johnston, Jesuit theologian, mystic, lifetime student of Zen Buddhism, once likened the devil to a chained dog. I had been reading one of his books, The Mirror Mind, before I left home and so he was in my thoughts. I wanted to tell him that this dog was a martyr in chains.

Although I was the only guest staying at the inn, the restaurant was full for the evening meal. One of the customers explained to me in French that the inn was famous for its fish cuisine and that he and his wife had driven fifty kilometres to dine here. I told him that I had walked over three hundred kilometres and was glad to hear the place was so good.

I had sword fish grilled on charcoal for my first course and then a delicious fish stew, mainly young eels, 'caldeira de enguias' which was the speciality of the house. The sweet course was a selection of elegant patisseries and the house wine a golden coloured Vinho Verde. Eating here was such a memorable experience, it seemed selfish to be on my own, not sharing such culinary delights.

In the front window of the restaurant, and all through the meal, a caged bird sang its heart out, singing sweetly, singing clearly, singing low.

> 'Beautiful must be the mountains whence ye come,
> And bright in the fruitful valleys the streams, where from
> Ye learnt your song:
> . . . .
> Nay, barren are those mountains and spent the streams:
> Our song is the song of desire, that haunts our dreams,' *

It was early next day when I set off south on a quiet road which followed the sandy spit parallel to the sea. It was a Sunday in the month of June, and only eighty kilometres from a big city, but there were no streams of cars, no hordes of picnickers, no fast food vans by the road side.

I reached Praia da Mira in the early afternoon and decided to take the rest of the day off, whether I had earned it or not. It was a quiet little seaside town, facing a sheltered lagoon with its back to the ocean.

I roamed the great sandy foreshore and sat on the beach watching the Atlantic rollers dash themselves on the shore. At their height, the crests

* from 'The Nightingales' by Robert Bridges

The beach at Praia da Mira

of the waves seemed so much higher than head height, it was amazing that the wash did not sweep up and cover the beach.

The boats had been pulled up on rollers, left above high tide line, ready for the fishing. They were sharp prowed, long and narrow, rising from a low stern to an elegant curved bow which reached away from the sea and pointed to the sky.

The traditional method of fishing is still used here, the boats built to be launched through the surf. Once beyond the breakers, the nets are cast and drawn in towards the shore. They are pulled up on the beach by oxen and the fishermen's helpers, men and women, young and old, the whole village turns out to share the labour as if by right.

The cool sound of huge waves falling on the shore was to stay with me for days, for days of hot walking on inland routes miles from the sea – as were the images of the caged bird and the chained dog. In some strange way both made me grateful for the freedom of wandering, aware that many a human life is as caged as the singing bird or as chained as the beautiful boxer dog.

CHAPTER 9

Roman Ruins at Conimbriga

The days were warmer now, much warmer. In Northern Portugal the weather had been as changeable as at home. But the temperatures were higher, even on the occasional dull mornings when the drizzle had settled on the land like a soft day in Ireland.

Now there seemed so little prospect of rain that the downpour on the last day across the mountains of Gerês might have happened on some previous trip. The heat rose by the day with the approach of full summer and as I walked, I searched for the shade.

I left the sea and Praia da Mira behind and strolled through forests rooted in sand towards the town of Mira. Between the clumps of trees there were small-holdings and in a field, courgettes grew at the base of maize plants, thriving in the shelter.

It was market day and I joined the trek to town. There were carts piled with produce, drawn by small horses or oxen, even cows had been harnessed between the shafts. Some people pushed hand carts or pulled a trailer behind a bicycle or a motor bike. There were vans packed so full, the back doors were held with rope, almost but not quite closed.

It was a cheerful throng, optimistic of selling their wares, certain it would be a good day out in the town. When we reached the centre it was full of people, pavements milling with adults and children, stalls being set up or already in action, trying to tempt customers, the bars and cafés crowded.

I joined them in a cup of coffee in a packed bar, my spirits as high as theirs. As I left, the customers waved and there were calls of encouragement.

When I was almost through the town, I met a woman selling sardines coming the other way. She was large and burly, no stranger to hard work, dressed in working black, her grey hair screwed back in a bun and an apron which reached down to her toes. She had obviously made one pass through the town and was now on her way back, determined not to miss a single sale.

The fish were piled on a rickety, make-shift trailer, built on the chassis of a baby's pram, with a large old-fashioned horn screwed to a bracket. The bulb of the horn was big but she had the hand to squeeze it.

She paused every few paces to send out a blast of noise which made the windows shake and then roared out in praise of her sardines.

Ten paces behind walked her teenage daughter, embarrassed, trying hard not to appear to be with her mother, but having been given no option but to be there. She was neatly dressed in blouse and shirt, her hair tied back with colourful ribbons. Once the work was done she would be hoping for her freedom in the town.

It was easy to see the relationship. They were the same strong, buxom build, the one frame twenty-odd years older and twenty-odd hard years of work wiser in the ways of the world. The mother kept glancing around in exasperation, annoyed that the girl was dawdling. When she looked back the daughter's attention was anywhere but on her mother.

I greeted the mother as we met and she laughed, brandishing a sardine under my nose and pretending to sell it to me to eat there and then. When I spoke to the daughter, she dropped her head in mortification as the great horn blasted out again and her mother's shouting filled the street with noise.

The route was flat, easy walking, often shaded. There were interesting villages and the small town of Cantanhede which was, as a complete contrast to Mira, almost deserted. Now that I was further south, was this siesta time? Or was everyone in Mira for the market? Near Coimbra, when I met the main road, the traffic increased to danger point for the walker and I waited for a bus into the town.

It was no surprise to find Coimbra, another of these small cities of Northern Portugal, such a fascinating and absorbing place to visit. I had come to expect something special. After all, I had been through Braga and Guimarães and even the huge city of Porto had been memorable.

On a long, solitary walk like this I was finding it pleasant to visit the cities with their concentration of life and energy, their history and art visible in their structures, their style and vitality accessible in their streets and cafés.

In spite of its size Porto had been no exception to this pattern, perhaps because of the old city within the vast conurbation. The smaller cities were ideal. Even on the shortest of visits I had a feeling that I had glimpsed their character, shared their life.

Coimbra is on a hill-side site overlooking the Rio Mondego. For almost two hundred years, through the 12th and 13th centuries, it was capital of Portugal. Its university is one of the oldest in the world. Its history has been carefully preserved in its buildings. Its romantic traditions in art, fado music and student life are still a part of the essence of the place.

It was the month of June so the students were very much in evidence.

In one large café more than half the tables were occupied by students at work, some studying on their own, others in serious discussion, books at hand, quotations being exchanged, notes being made. I had a feeling that examinations were imminent.

There appeared to be no pressure on the students to order something to eat or drink. They seemed to be here as if by right, their privacy respected by the staff and the other customers.

The romantic traditions are still part of the lives of the students here. They sing the fado and play guitars. They sport ribbons on their cases to denote their faculties. Some form groups, known as republics of about twelve students from the same locality and live communally, sharing lodgings and cooking together.

I found a room in a small, comfortable pensão and ate well in the dining room. The inn's reputation for food must have been good, for the room was full of locals who gave the impression that they knew what they were about.

It was a small room and the one other foreigner was English. He too was a traveller, a stranger in town and he greeted me in a cockney accent. But it was not me he wanted to talk to. He spoke Portuguese, to my untutored ear, fluently and he addressed the staff and the other diners at length, whether or not they wanted to listen, showing off his skill.

His audience showed patience and the usual courtesy, but no interest in what he was saying. It was hardly because he was English. Unlike some other European countries, being English would appear to be no disadvantage in Portugal.

It was such a surprise, that I wanted to ask him what he had said, in order to understand why he had left them so indifferent, but he ate quickly and left.

Later some of the patrons spoke to me and when I answered with my few hard-won, halting words in their language they showed considerable interest in my journey, questioning me at length. It was intriguing and had my command of Portuguese been better, I would have been tempted to ask why they had reacted so un-sympathetically to the Englishman.

In the morning I crossed the Rio Mondego, my fourth River of Portugal and, unwilling to face the traffic on the main road connecting Lisbon and Porto, reputedly one of the busiest roads in the country, I took the bus to Condeixa. It was a detour, further west than I needed to go but three or four kilometres from Condeixa is the Roman site of Conimbriga. Since my visit to the Celtic village of Citânia de Briteiros I had been looking forward to seeing Conimbriga, remains of the same era but of a very different culture.

Café at Coimbra

The entrance to the site let me walk another stretch of Roman road, this time part of the route from Braga to Lisbon, for Conimbriga was a major staging post on that journey.

Conimbriga is the largest and perhaps the most important Roman site in Portugal. In its heyday it was a summer resort. There is a massive wall confusingly built through the remains of the town, as if added at a later stage in time of danger.

There are pools and fountains amongst the ruins and beautiful mosaic floors. There are fine houses once carefully planned and constructed and, no doubt, exceedingly comfortable. A forum still stands, ready for use. The focal point of the site is the magnificent baths complex with hundreds of water inlets and an elaborate underfloor heating system, now exposed by the excavations.

The time saved by taking the bus let me spend the entire morning wandering around the site, sitting on ancient steps to feel the spirit that had once made this place alive, sketching its pillars and walls, stone set upon stone. Over two thousand years ago this was part of an empire which carried its civilization to the furthest corners of Europe.

It was an atmospheric place, but in a very different way from Briteiros. That Celtic village had moved me. I was affected in some mystical way which I could sense but not articulate, even to myself. Here, the town of Conimbriga was a dramatic revelation of the talents, ingenuity and effort of those who had served the great Roman Empire. I was impressed, aware of being privileged to be here.

I travelled on in the early afternoon. The sky was cloudless, the heat rising to the hottest day yet. The quiet road led south-east through flat terrain at first, dulled by the blazing sun to hazy skylines and empty, uninteresting fields. I reached a minor road and, as it climbed into the shade of a fir forest, the road became no more than a country lane. The view brightened, looking out from under the shadows to horizons miles away It was good walking.

The fir trees gave way to cork oak, gnarled and twisted as if pollarding had spoiled their natural form. The shade was good and I strolled on into the late afternoon. I was enjoying myself here but a glance at the map showed me that it was still a long way to go to Figueiró dos Vinhos, the next village that might be big enough to have an inn. In the excitement of the visit to the Roman site, and for the first time on the trip, I had not bothered to add up the total kilometres for the day's projected route.

My mind was sluggish from the heat and I was still contemplating this omission when I came out on a narrow road. Almost immediately a van stopped beside me. The driver was delivering cakes to village shops and he insisted I sample his wares as he gave me a lift towards Figueiró. He stopped at the bottom of a gorge, pointed to the hills and told me there was a fine inn in the village.

The impossible had been made possible. I was within ten kilometres of Figueiró, walking up the narrow road as it followed the twists of the gorge. There were huge straight-trunked eucalyptus trees amongst the cork oaks and firs. The river tumbled down in its chasm. The air was warm, heavily scented by the trees. The eucalyptus dominated, then the fir. There was no traffic either up or down the road. The birds sang, as if for me, no more beautifully than the caged bird in Praia da Mira, but free.

I arrived in Figueiró dos Vinhos in the early evening. The van driver was right. There was a good inn and, under a cool flow of a powerful shower, I eased the heat of the day from my bent head and neck. I raised my arms to the water, revelling in it like a Roman bather. It cascaded over my shoulders and trunk and, last of all, I let it pour down on my upturned face.

Figueiró was the sort of place I took to right away. A large café and bar on the main street was set on a raised stone base. It sported huge banners proclaiming its special significance in the revolution of the 25 April 1974, when an army coup d'état ousted the Salazar regime. When the soldiers occupied Lisbon, they did so with flowers stuck in the barrels of their rifles. It was the Carnation Revolution.

In other parts of the country, the revolution was not so peacefully achieved. There was no indication of what had happened in Figueiró except that the change had been of such momentous significance that it required to be remembered with pride, and in full view of all who came here.

The size and prominence of these revolutionary slogans gave Figueiró an air of independence, perhaps even truculence, which rested easily on the place. Perched high in the hills, amongst the most beautiful countryside, Figueiró seemed somehow distanced from the rest of the country, a frontier town where order and policy were now local affairs, not imposed by outsiders and from afar.

It was so easy to find a room at the inn, I could hardly credit now how difficult it had been two weeks before to ask for a bed for the night. As I strolled around the town in the early evening the locals spoke to me with quiet dignity, seemingly pleased to see a stranger in their streets. Figueiró is famous for its pottery and the displays outside shops are a feature of the town.

Later I went to the revolutionary café to eat and, as I entered saw an earthenware dish in the local style being carried to a table. The contents had such an appetising smell that there was no need of a menu to help me choose my main course.

It was one of the many forms of bacalhau, the cod fish dishes which are so essential to the cuisine of Northern Portugal. The cod is dried and stored salted, and must be steeped in three or more changes of water before use. I had tried the bacalhau on three or four other evenings without finding it particularly to my taste, but this version was the speciality of the house and I decided to give the salted cod one last chance to prove its worth.

For once patience was rewarded. The bacalhau arrived in an impressive dish, hot enough to make the air quiver, and I was warned not to touch. The fish had been baked with small potatoes and whole onions, flavoured with herbs and garlic, and covered in sauce. It had been crisped on its surface at the last stages of the cooking.

I served myself from the earthenware dish and the bacalhau was delicious, just the style of a meal I needed at the end of another long day's walking. The local wine was a light shade of red, fresh, smelling of fruit and no surprise to me to find it so good with the fish.

The staff watched my obvious enjoyment of the bacalhau with pleasure and pretended astonishment when they discovered that I had eaten the full of the casserole. The cook came out, smiling broadly, to ask if I could manage some more. But I shook his hand in congratulation and declined.

In the morning I left Figueiró dos Vinhos feeling that this was yet another place where I could happily dwell for a while. Most long-distance walkers give the impression of being driven onwards by the need to do the distance of the day, to get the journey finished, over and done with. As if to feel the desire to linger is a sin against the purity of the achievement.

Time and distance are of the essence. A bus ride or a lift are heresies they would never countenance. One whose writings I admire because of the way he can reveal his thoughts, amazed me recently by saying that while others may claim to meet all sorts of interesting people on their journeys, it never happens to him.

My journey was now in its own stride and ahead was Tomar, just north of the great Rio Tagus, the river that rises in the very heart of Spain and cuts Portugal in two.

The route south was far from direct, but through the shade of forests, meandering between the hills. It struck me that, although the countryside was just as afforested here as further north and a great deal drier, I had not seen a burned out forest since I crossed the Rio Douro.

I sat down for a rest in a woodland glade near a bridge which spanned the river in the depths of a gorge. My perch was high enough to let me see villages perched on hill tops. Below the gorge, where it twisted into the lower land, there were wooded hills forcing the tributary streams to bend and loop around them.

I could hear the water falling over rocks, gurgling between the stones. The birds sang, calling louder, trilling more insistently, singing with more variety of song than on any other day.

The place constructed its own meditation for me. Calm and peaceful, but neither silent nor still. Where were the strains and stresses of life now? Even the immediate difficulties of my way of travelling seemed inconsequential, the kilometres to be walked on tired feet, the distances between inns, my lack of fluency in the language.

My spirits rose and I walked on, feeling happier with my journey than on any previous day so far.

These forests were obviously an important local resource. Each one seemed to have its own team of workmen, felling, clearing, tending the woods. In one pine forest, each tree had been cut carefully to let the resin flow. At the base of the cut there was a flowerpot shaped bowl to collect the sticky liquid. I met a man clearing the bowls and we exchanged greetings, shyly but both glad to have someone to speak to.

Now I was much further south, I began to think about the burned out forests in the north. They were the most bleak and desolate places I had passed through, without a sign of animal or plant life. There were so many of them in the north and I knew that most of the fires had been started deliberately. Apparently a burned forest makes the charcoal sellers job much easier. But there appeared to be other reasons, political reasons.

At election time the socialist left, the ruling party, claim that the forests are burned by right wingers to show that law and order has broken down. The right claim that it is the left who do the burning, to prove the country is so poor that men must destroy the woodlands to provide work.

A government campaign is now underway to persuade the people that the burning of forests is an evil which blights the countryside. For the future of those areas in the north, the campaign must succeed.

In a café in the village of Cabacos two men took the trouble to talk to me slowly and distinctly, hoping I would understand. One had worked on an oil rig and he was critical of his village, so contemptuous I wondered why he stayed. The other was the owner of the bar and he was gentle, helpful, telling me that Tomar, where I was bound, was a wonderful town.

A boy showed me his disfigured hands, not for sympathy, or reward, but just to let me see them.

Hours later I entered Tomar and the pavement I walked on was paved, terazzo style. The background was white and the motif, large blue Maltese crosses. At that moment the significance of these splayed crosses eluded me but later, all was revealed.

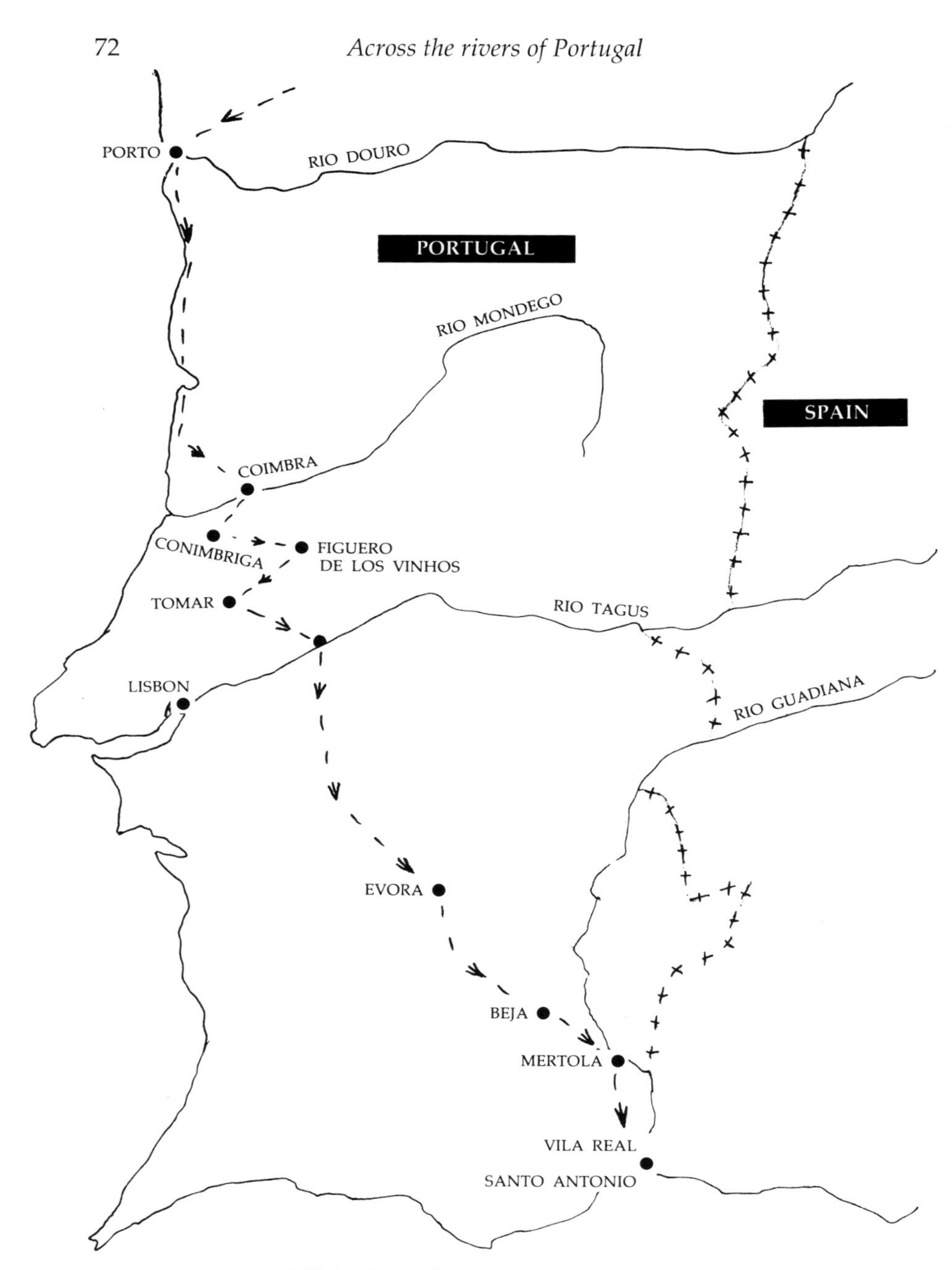

MAP 3 – From the River Tagus to the Algarve

CHAPTER 10

Templar Ghosts

Stepping on the Maltese crosses was the strangest of sensations, as if it might be irreverent, as if I should keep to the plain tiles, like a youngster taking the greatest care to keep off the lines between the pavement flagstones.

It was not the fact that they were crosses. At my school, the game of rugby was revered to the extent that success on the field of play was on a par with the very highest academic achievement. Once established on the school First XV, the player was entitled to have a large Maltese cross sewn on the front of his jersey. The crosses were white on blue jerseys, later changed to blue on white, as on this pavement. At that age, and within that sphere, the Maltese cross was worn as a proud symbol of sporting endeavour. The strange sensation was to come upon it so unexpectedly in Tomar and the connection back to my youth was so strong, that it kept the significance of its presence here from my mind.

I found a room at a pensão and in the late afternoon followed a path paved with small stones up the steep hill above the town. It was an ancient roadway flanked by small lighting towers and it curved around the hill to make the upward struggle easier.

It reached a sheer sweep of massive walls, presumably enclosing the summit of the hill and so high I could see only glimpses of the castle within. Surprisingly, the car park to my right, presumably reached by a modern road, was empty except for one large tour bus.

The gates in the wall were open and I strolled through the complex of protective archways and came out before a magnificent castle. No crumbling ruin this, it was a magnificent fortress, looking as firm and solid as the day it was built.

A uniformed official approached and, assuming I was French, told me in that language that, as it was a public holiday, the castle was closed to visitors. He explained that the gates had been opened only because the party in the tour bus had made a special arrangement to be allowed inside the grounds. The castle itself, however, would remain closed.

He chatted to me in friendly fashion, as if glad to have someone to talk to as we walked towards where the group had assembled. They were supposed to be listening to their guide but they were paying no heed to him. There was a great deal of agitated talking, with theatrical shrugs and gestures of frustration and then the shouts of criticism began. The guide was probably Portuguese and flushed with embarrassment at the rudeness of his charges.

'You are not French?' whispered the official to me loudly and in that language, and not really needing a reply. He smiled when I nodded agreement and nudged me with his elbow.

'They are French of course. Look at them. They are mad.' He was obviously amused at the antics of these thwarted tourists without the slightest sympathy for their plight. 'They have come a long way to see the Convento do Cristo and now it is closed. They are blaming the guide.'

They were all men in the group, late thirties to sixties, exceedingly well-dressed in light-weight suits, or elegantly casual in designer sweaters or jackets and slacks. Boorish behaviour is even less attractive in smart clothes.

One of the Frenchmen began to imitate the guide, pretending to read from a book hidden inside his jacket, mocking the guide's stance and accent. The others laughed and began to wander away back to the bus, leaving the guide to continue his talk on the great Convento to ever dwindling numbers.

I gathered from what was said, that the tour party could not stay until the next day, but that was their problem. I had intended to do my weekly broadcast in the morning and leave the town, heading south, immediately afterwards. Now I decided to stay to see the castle the next afternoon and spend a second night in Tomar.

That evening, on the river bank, I sat by the lake, sharing the friendliness of the people as they strolled in the warmth of the June evening, and later took my ease amongst the streets of this charming old town.

Next day I made my broadcast from the pensão, telling the tale of the lost sole and the chain of helpfulness begun by the kindness of the retired fisherman.

In the afternoon, I climbed the steep path again to the Convento do Cristo and met my friend, the uniformed official, at the pay desk in the gateway.

The Convent of Christ was unlike any castle I had ever seen before. Its state of preservation was so good, it seemed built for some recent age, although its walls were erected in the 12th century.

It is a monumental construction on the summit of the hill, traditionally one of the first seats of the Knights Templar. Beyond the imposing entrance is the nave. The cloisters are calm and uncluttered, the simple

The Castle of the Knights Templar at Tomar

decoration in contrast to the intricate ornamentation of the nave and chapter house.

This Manueline style of complex carving in stone was new to me, the motifs woven together, their finest details illustrated like twisted strands of rope, brocaded cloth, fret-worked wood, instead of solid rock.

There are such stunning examples of this style, perhaps the Frenchmen were a group of architects on a study tour, coming to Tomar to see the famous Manueline Window, only to be foiled by the inconvenient closure of the castle on a Public Holiday.

The Templar Order was formed in the early years of the 12th century by crusader knights in Jerusalem, to protect pilgrims on the way to the holy places. In Spain and Portugal, their main purposes were to help in the reconquest of those lands from the Moors and to protect pilgrims on the way to the shrine of St. James at Santiago de Compostela.

The Convento do Cristo was founded by Gualdim Pais, one of the grandest masters of the order and it became renowned as their religious and military headquarters. By the end of the 13th century, the wealth, influence and power of the Templars was such that others in the very highest positions, most notably the King of France, Philippe-le-Bel, coveted their proud place in the Christian world.

The enemies of the Order grew in strength and confidence, when the Archbishop of Bordeaux was elected Pope Clement the Fifth. At the beginning of the 14th century, and on his orders, the suppression of the Templars began in France in a fury of torture, hanging and burning at the stake.

Surviving knights, particularly from Spain, sought refuge in Portugal, where the king, Dom Denis, reconstituted the Order as the Knights of Christ. The new Order inherited the lands and wealth of the Templars but were now under the leadership and control of the throne.

During the next two hundred years, the Order prospered and was involved in financing the great Voyages of Discovery. The ships carried their emblem, the splayed cross I knew as the Maltese Cross, on their sails. This link, between the Templars and the development of the Portuguese Empire, is clear in the design of the Manueline Window, for it includes masts, ropes, seaweed and anchor chains and the bust of a sea captain.

Here in the Convento I heard the voice of a guide droning quietly behind a pillar. There were few visitors, all seemed to be in a guided group or hanging on its edges, listening to the words of wisdom. I waited until they had finished in the Charola before I made my move.

The Charola was built by the Templars in the 12th century to be a replica of the Holy Sepulchre in Jerusalem. It is almost circular, a sixteen-sided chapel, the sacred heart of the Convento. There are alcoves around the wall, each big enough to accommodate a man on a horse. The legend is that the knights attended mass on horseback. The place has an aura, beyond usual Christian practice, which allows this to seem plausible.

In the centre of the chapel is the high altar, itself surrounded by pillars in a tight octagon.

The visitors were in some other part of the complex, the officials elsewhere too. I sat down on the base of one of the pillars in the centre of this strange, atmospheric sanctuary. A bird flew around the Charola, without panic, in no hurry to escape to the freedom of the open air, used to being here, I supposed.

Had there been anyone else about I might have felt too self-conscious to sit here on this smooth stone plinth, meditating, back against the pillar, body still, mind calm, spirit at ease, as if this was in the nature of this place.

Wherever I travel in Europe, the Templars seem to have been there before me. Without seeking out their sites, my routes bring me to their doorsteps. Lacking any great knowledge of their history and having no connection with organisations which may trace their origins to the Order, like the Freemasons, I find myself in their ancient haunts.

Once, in my early years as a teacher, a colleague, with the very best of intentions, but without my knowledge, put me up for election to a Masonic Lodge. I was black-balled and my colleague's disappointment was only equalled by my relief at not being elected. Had I been accepted, I would, without clearly knowing why, have felt compelled to refuse the invitation to join and thus compounded my colleague's mortification.

But here I was where the knights had worshipped, by some accounts dealing in the Occult as well as Christianity. The home of 'Christ's Malitia', sworn to poverty, chastity and obedience, independent and proud. Some said they were heretical, beyond the laws of state or God, outside the rule of the Pope himself, too arrogant, too proud, too interested in power.

As it was, no one entered the Charola while I was there, nor did I feel they would. The sensation was not that this site was sacred in a particularly Christian way, but there was a mystical feeling of strength and power, which crossed the centuries effortlessly, as if by divine right.

As in the Celtic village, I had no sense of having been here before but the familiarity was uncanny. I seemed to know its ghosts. They were making me welcome, not surprised that I was here, knowing that I would not be misled by the myths of history, expecting me to understand.

I sat at ease where the warrior monks had once held sway and let a tiny coin from home roll through a crack at the base of the pillar and drop into the very foundations of the Charola. A traveller's mite to join the vast wealth of the Templars. I knew it might seem ludicrously inconsequential, even foolish, amongst such monumental images, but at the time I needed to leave some token here.

On the Road to Santiago I had found my meditations in spiritual places become prayer, as if they were one and the same. A friend of mine, whose calling requires and enables her to spend a great deal more time in prayer than most, describes her praying as talking to God.

Here, my contemplation was unlike any form of prayer I knew. My spirit seemed intimate with the air of the Charola, my mind alive with its images, not dramatic representations in vivid detail, like 19th century portrait painters but impressions as strong as the paintings of Monet or Pissarro.

There was no need to separate fact of history from myth. No need to believe or disbelieve. It was enough to be here.

The reputation of sites like the Convento do Cristo draws us to see them but we need calm and quiet enough to allow ourselves the time to feel their aura. Modern life rarely leaves us time for such opportunities but they are there for the taking, like visiting an art gallery to appreciate just one picture or allowing a piece of music to reach beyond our hearing, or sitting alone amongst ancient ruins, letting the day move on as the mind drifts back in time.

CHAPTER 11

Gipsy Friends

I left the Convento do Cristo by the main gate, in danger of leaving my spirit behind. The car park was almost empty, its dirt surface carefully swept free of the inevitable litter of tourism in such places.

But the old cobbled road to the town, as it curved steeply downwards, was ankle deep in debris and I waded through it, kicking coke tins and crisp bags from under my feet. Why was the car park so clean? Had the rubbish been conveniently blown here by the wind or dumped over the parapet by the cleaners?

Surprisingly, the sight of this ancient path being treated so contemptuously when the Convento itself was so carefully preserved, made me much less angry than it had done on the way up the previous day.

Then the route to the castle had seemed, in its own way, as significant as the massive walls and I had been incensed that the authorities had allowed it to become a rubbish dump. Now I took a more tolerant view. Who would want to travel the modern road to and from the car park at the gate when this cobbled way could be walked? The refuse of the last few metres seemed a small price to pay to step back in time, to tread where the Templar Knights and their steeds had trod.

I left Tomar reluctantly in the morning and an old man directed me out of the town with courtesy and pride.

'Para onde via?' he said. 'Where are you going?'

'Abrantes' I pronounced the name of the town I was heading for as confidently as I could, having heard it said in Tomar.

'Abrantes!' the old man said loudly, eyebrows raised in approval, not afraid to let the world hear him speak. 'Abrantes! Abrantes!' he roared, rolling the words as he spoke, letting the sound ring down the street, cheering me on.

The little roads and paths took me through miles of woods to a huge dam on the Rio Zezere and I crossed at its outlet. A dusty track led directly south through dry lands, with clumps of pine and stretches of olive trees,spaced widely to use what moisture there was in the soil.

This was so unlike any part of the countryside I had yet travelled through. It was a parched land, with tiny settlements well separated from each other, fenced and walled as if for protection.

The off-white dust on the surface of the way squeaked under my feet and rose in eddies with each faint puff of wind. I could feel the heat of the day drying my system to the point of dehydration. There were little settlements, splashes of brilliant white against terrain of palest brown.

It should have been possible to replenish my water bottles but all the dwellings had their shuttered backs to the road. There was no one about, no door to knock, no obvious way in. I licked my lips with the tip of my tongue and kept my mouth closed to keep the moisture in.

All through the afternoon, I kept going steadily, without hurry, carefully trying to save the little energy I had by moving in the most economical way. In the distance a cloud of white dust moved slowly towards me. It was a four-wheel drive pick-up truck, bouncing along the path. The driver waved and slowed almost to stalling point to reduce the cloud of dust. I turned away, my face covered with my shirt front and tried to stop breathing until he was well past.

The track came to a road at a small village and I had the luxury of a seat in the shade, in a bar. It was a hard, upright chair and it was a very simple establishment but it seemed luxurious to me. I ordered bottles of cold orange and a coffee, drinking one in great draughts and the other in sips between the swigs. Cold orange and warm coffee may seem like a weird combination but at this moment it was perfect. The one quenched my body's thirst and the other revived my mind.

The road was near the Rio Tejo, the great River Tagus which rises near Madrid in the very heart of Spain and flows into the Atlantic near Lisbon. I was now amongst the woods and olive groves again and blessed shade as tiredness slowed me to a stroll.

I saw Abrantes perched on a hill in the distance, white houses covering the slopes, a fortress on the summit. By the time I reached its streets it had been another twenty-mile day and felt as if it had been much longer.

But in the streets, as narrow as alleyways, my spirits rose and the tiredness fell away. The people seemed so cheerful, calling to each other in voices that could have been heard at the other end of the town. The houses were festooned with flowers in bloom, such flashes of colour against the white stone.

The inn was in the oldest part of the town, where a narrow street opened into a square. Its entrance, at street level, was a wide archway which led up a flight of steps to the door on the first floor. I rang the bell and waited. After a decent interval, there were scuffling sounds above accompanied by loud sighs and grunts, as someone moved inside.

The door opened and a senhora stood there, hands on hips, eyeing me. She looked me up and down before she spoke, even in greeting.

'Bom dia.' I said, to fill the space. 'Queria um quarto.' 'I'd like a room.' It was just as well I felt fairly confident of the words. Had I been confronted by this formidable senhora during the first few days of my trip I would surely have failed to make my simple needs understood.

She ignored my request and ordered me to ascend the stone steps. As there was obviously no chance of her coming down to talk to me, I obeyed. Once I was inside her front door she became a different woman. I was now in her care and she treated me with friendly tolerance.

The inn itself was an old building, well cared for, lovingly preserved. The doors and bannisters were fine, polished dark wood, the walls and ceilings clean white plaster.

The senhora padded along in front of me, talking to herself as she climbed the stairs at her own speed, bursting into little snatches of song, looking around to smile at me, now I was her guest. A woman happy in work and life, I would have guessed.

There were antique fitments and furnishings, everything neatly in its place. Through a glass door I saw a banty cock and hens on the first floor patio, scratching amongst the seeds of grain, as happy as their mistress.

My room was reached through the kitchen and was on the second floor. It was large and simply comfortable, clean and polished, cool and bright. There was an enamel wash basin and a jug on the marble wash stand. In a corner stood an elaborate wooden clothes stand that would have been at home in a gentleman's dressing room and at the window was a fine writing desk which would have graced his study. I could have made myself comfortable here for a week.

I was the only guest and the staff were engaged on the chores of spring cleaning. There were three of them, all girls in their late teens or early twenties. They were painting a room near mine, chatting to each other, calling to their friends in the street. The spirit moved one of them and she began to sing a slow, sad fado song with a voice of such power and assuredness that it filled the inn with sound.

In the heart of Portugal I had found a place to stay which was all I might have hoped for, comfortable, congenial, a true traveller's rest.

In the early evening the day cooled, the tiredness receded and I climbed the hill to the castle, not energetically, but with a far more sprightly step than I could have hoped for when arriving in Abrantes.

The battlements were on the grand scale and the view magnificent, great ranges of mountains to the north, rolling countryside to the south, covered with vast plantations of olive trees and tiny white villages still showing brightly in the evening light.

This was a true vantage point, dominating the land and the Rio

Tagus. No wonder this site had been an important stronghold of the Romans and the Moors or that General Wellesley, who, of course, after the event became the Duke of Wellington, made his headquarters here during the Peninsular War.

From my perch on the walls, it was easy to believe that he who occupied this fortress could command the very heart of Portugal.

Later I ate in a restaurant recommended in the Rough Guide as 'one of the most stylish restaurants in all Portugal'. The owner surprised me by speaking English. It was the first time I had been asked for my order in that language since I left Santiago at the beginning of my walk.

He recommended 'Carne de Porco a Alentejana', a dish from the next region I was to travel through. I took his advice. It proved to be pork and cockles, cooked in a creamy, pale brown sauce, tender and succulent, the distinctive flavours of the meat and the shellfish both evident, neither one dominated by the other. The wine was a white from the region, a Chamusca, stronger than the Vinho Verde, flavoursome and refreshing.

Abrantes is famous for its desserts and I had an elegant confection of pastry and sweet egg straws. A walker can enjoy such a treat and, indeed, have a second helping, without the conscience nagging on about calories or cholesterol or putting on the extra pounds. In fact, the very reverse is true. My previous long-distance journey had taught me that I must eat exceedingly well to keep going over the weeks of walking. With meals like this, it was no hardship.

An old man sat near me, well dressed, obviously at his usual table. The owner and he knew each other's ways and he read as he picked at his food. Two families shared two tables, the adults at one, the children at the other, each table having a life of its own.

A young couple with a very young child smiled across the room and tried to talk to me. At this stage my Portuguese was adequate for ordering a meal or asking for a room but, sadly, not up to conversation. But we had recognised each other and passed the time of day.

They made me feel welcome in the genuine way that I had met throughout my trip. It had nothing to do with formal good manners, but was simple friendliness and the acceptance of a stranger in their place. They asked me where I was from and when the answer was 'Ireland' their response was, as invariably it had been since I crossed the border, 'Irlanda do Norte' and spoken with knowing nods.

Before I left, I complimented the owner on the meal and asked him if the recommendation in the Rough Guide had been good for business. He was not able to hide his irritation.

'No!' he said testily. 'I wish my restaurant had never been mentioned.

It has brought those with no interest in Portuguese food, expecting American or French cooking, expecting to pay nothing.'

I smiled in understanding and he began to laugh, now the outburst had let the anger out of his system.

'Fortunately, few of them reach Abrantes.' he said with a grin. 'I must learn to take my holidays in the summer, so that we are closed when they come.'

I left the restaurant and strolled the streets in the warm evening air. Abrantes was quieter now. When I arrived it had been alive with sound. The Portuguese are often cheerful, exuberant, given to loud conversations with their friends in the street. They choose an archway for a chat, as the sound reverberates like an echo chamber. They talk to each other across the street, bantering their friends from windows or café doorways. Families whoop and yell at each other in recognition.

That afternoon I had realised that the language was not designed for surreptitious conversations, whispered asides, quiet confidences. It worked best at volume, spoken with power and conviction. A tongue unafraid to let the world know what it was saying.

But that had been earlier, now Abrantes was a gentler place, as if the day was drawing to a close. I stopped to speak to a gipsy family and gave them a few coins as we parted. The woman took them with dignity, as if they were her right.

Later two small boys approached me, hands outstretched and she called them off with one roar from the far end of the street, that stopped them in their tracks like a stun gun. I smiled at the boys as they turned away and the woman and I exchanged cheery waves. It was like a seal of acceptance here.

In the morning the day started hot and, although I was away early, the preparations for a fair had already begun. People were arriving in their hundreds at a site on the edge of the town, near the river. They came by bus, lorry, pick-up truck and carts drawn by horse or mule.

The crowd was so dense, I could hardly find the bridge over the Rio Tagus. I passed the clothes stalls and found my way through the meals section, doing a great breakfast trade.

Crossing the bridge I almost forgot to drop my small coin into the great flow of the Tagus, such was the excitement around me. On the far side there was some shade and dozens of mules were tethered, as if every mule and jennet in central Portugal had been brought here for the fair.

I left it all reluctantly, but I had started on the way to the Alentejo and there was no pausing now.

A quiet country road led south into the heat of the day. There was no traffic for the first hour and I walked on the right hand side, where a line of trees gave intermittent shade. The contrast to the noise and bustle of the fair was total, the only sounds, bird song and the crunch of my feet on the gravel at the side of the road.

In the distance behind me, I heard the rattle of a motorbike engine. I knew that raucous, staccato beat. There had been days when it had stalked me across the countryside, like the death rattle of an ancient tractor.

The Portuguese sometimes remove the silencers from their bikes in the belief, an engineer friend tells me, and unlikely as it seems, that it saves petrol.

The rattle became a roar. I looked around and approaching at a slow, stately speed was a gipsy astride an old bike, with a tiny helmet perched on his head, like half an orange crowning a melon.

The bike drew level and I could see that one reason for the slow speed was that it was towing a ramshackle trailer as big as a kitchen table. The trailer was packed with people. Two women and a crowd of children of all ages and sizes were squeezed in between the board sides.

There was a shout of recognition from amongst the passengers. It was the same family I had met on the previous evening, now packed together with their friends, enjoying a day out.

One of the women leant forward and yelled something in the driver's ear. He shook his great head from side to side so vehemently I was afraid his helmet would fall off. Dissatisfied by this reply, the two women began to beat him on the back with their fists. They had the advantage of him. He was not able to let go the handlebars to turn around and defend himself. They could pound him at will.

Eventually, he could take no more and with a monumental shrug of the shoulders, he steered the bike and trailer in a graceful U-turn and came back towards me. As they passed, the passengers cheered and he glowered at me, not with malice, I presumed, but because, and quite understandably, he hated being told what to do by the women.

Another elegant U-turn brought the outfit back in my direction and it stopped beside me. I took it that the cries of encouragement were offers of a lift, but the trailer was so packed, there was no room for my rucksac, never mind me. There was a deal of jostling and pushing and a tiny space appeared at the back. I pointed at my feet.

'A pé!' I shouted above the din. 'Obrigado! A pé! A pé!' 'Thank you. I'm on foot!'

There were shouts of disbelief and hands reached out to help me on board. I shook my head and lifted a foot to show them.

'A pé! A pé!' I roared. 'Obrigado! Obrigado!'

A small boy jumped down and slapped me on the back. The others raised their fists in the air and cheered. I shook hands with everyone I could reach and the driver gave a loud grunt, as he pulled slowly away. He lifted both hands from the handlebars and raised his arms to the sky in a gesture of resignation at the folly of women and children and the stupidity of the stranger, refusing a lift.

The cheering and waving continued until they were out of sight. They left me laughing aloud to myself. They had brought me a moment of true happiness.

For me, an important part of the solo journeys has been the experience of being on my own, for long periods at a time. The silence and the time to think have been a revelation. Travelling in these countries on foot, staying at small inns, has given me the privilege of feeling accepted by the local people, not as an affluent visitor but as a simple traveller in their land. It came to mind at the time, that in Ireland, gipsies are often known as travellers too.

Had they thought it worth thinking about, these gipsies would, at best, have placed me on the same rung of the social ladder as themselves, perhaps a rung or two lower, for they had wheels and I was on my feet.

Uriah Heep gave humility a bad name. In modern life, there seems little place for what was once esteemed as a virtue. The fact is, however, that like solitude, most of us are the better for a touch of it.

We were travelling at different speeds, but their spirit remained with me every step of the way to my resting place at the end of the day and beyond that to the very end of my journey.

CHAPTER 12

Old Bones and the Town Dog in Evora

When I reached Pont de Sor, I felt myself relaxing in a great surge, as if my whole body had breathed a sigh of relief. It was a very small town, more a village, but it seemed that it was the centre for a huge area of countryside.

The inn was the grandest I had yet stayed in, perched beside the bridge over the Rio Sor. The river was in a deep cleft, the surrounding wooded hills and valleys idyllic. The terrace of the inn was spacious, tables either in the sun or shade, a fine vantage point for the view and a grandstand seat for the action around the bridge. The inn at Pont de Sor had a self-confident air, an important place for afternoons off, for holiday week-ends, the hub of an important inland resort.

Room and dinner were good value and I ate well in the evening. The caldo verde was an appetizing potato and cabbage soup and the hake grilled to perfection with garlic and butter and served with small, new potatoes. Later I wandered through the village, easing out tired legs. The locals recognised me as a stranger, and smiled and moved over to make a space for me at a crowded pavement café.

That night I opened the bedroom windows as usual but slept only fitfully. My room was at the front of the inn and, although the traffic was light, two or three times an hour a car or a motor bike would speed past. Each driver announced his arrival at the bridge with a horn blast, like the whistle shriek of a steam train about to enter a tunnel.

It was too hot a night to close the windows – better to be disturbed than stifled, I thought – as I was wakened yet again by a motorbike's roar reverberating in the river's chasm.

I dreamed dark, depressing dreams. Their stories eluded me when I was startled awake enough to be able to think. After a pleasant evening it was a shock to be in such a melancholy mood. The dejection was at its worst in that uncertain, vulnerable hour before night gives way to dawn. It was still with me when I left in the morning and tagged along as I walked south to Montargil.

It was another hot day, my first in the Alentejo. I was expecting the heat, and had been told that the air would be dry, not humid, but as I walked, it became the most sultry, sticky day I had ever experienced.

I followed a lake for miles, plugging on without pleasure, the sweat running down my face and body, soaking my shirt instead of drying on the skin. I spotted a bar in a small village, crowded with men. It should have been an oasis and I eased my way through the mob to the counter to order a cool orange drink.

The girl was busy and, so stiflingly oppressive was the atmosphere, I had to leave before she could bring my order. Outside, there was no shade and I had to walk on, feeling badly done by, sorry for myself, cheated of my drink.

When I walk or climb with others I suppose I would be the one who usually tries to keep the others cheerful, who looks on the bright side, at my best when things go wrong. Be that true or false, now I was the one in need of a companion, a soul mate who would understand, who would brighten the day and shorten the journey with merry chat. But I was alone, a stranger in a strange land, with not enough words of the language for conversation with the locals.

On all my solo walking, this was only the second time I had been so affected. On the Road to Santiago, I had experienced uncomfortable loneliness for the first few days. Then, although the days had been wonderful, I had been the only guest at the inns and the only one to dinner. Afterwards, a friend had said that there had been so much to share and no one to share it with.

Now it was different. Although the experiences of the journey were just as enthralling, I was much further along the way, when the dark, unremembered dreams of this one night had led to depressing thoughts in the day. They brought doubts about the purpose of the journey, my motives for undertaking it, about my strength of body and spirit to complete it, about the relevance of the journey to my life's quest, about its significance for anyone other than myself.

As I faced the doubts and fears they wriggled away, one by one, not wishing to be so confronted, hoping not to be forced out into the open. But even when I had dealt with all of them, my spirits were still low. On such a journey, it feels right for me to travel on my own, but this was different. Now all I needed was a companion to cheer me on the way.

In other circumstances, the walk to Montargil might have been a delight, but not on this day. I found a small inn near the town and grumpily insisted on a quiet room away from the road.

I was the only one to dinner but the boy who served me was friendly and the food was good. Reluctantly, my good spirits began to return, a little at a time. A huge tureen of soup helped right the body's liquid balance and as it restored me physically, I realised that part of the day's depression had probably been the first effects of heat exhaustion.

The main course was 'Cabrito assado no forno', the flesh of young goat in a casserole, succulent and tender. The salad could not have been simpler – tomatoes, onions and cucumber – but the onions were full of flavour without being sharp, the cucumber thinly sliced and ripe. It was the tomatoes, however, which made the meal. They were slices from that large, oddly shaped variety we unimaginatively call beefsteak tomatoes, which look under-ripe because the skin may be more green than red, but taste delicious. I was refreshed by the meal as well as replenished.

That night my dreams were dull but not dark or disturbing, as if my mind was shedding its excess baggage. I wakened in the last hour before dawn again but the first light chased the doubts and fears, 'the stone that puts the stars to flight'.

Again it was hot early and humid as I walked south in the morning. I passed through groves of peach trees with wooden structures for collecting and sorting the fruit at the road side. A lorry load of girls, dressed alike in head scarves, long skirts and Wellington boots, arrived to pick and sort the peaches and they called to me, their shouts sounding like encouragement.

The day was long and very hard in the conditions. Surprisingly the need to keep going prevented me from becoming as dejected as the previous day. It seemed to concentrate my effort.

After seventeen miles or so I reached a village with a comfortable, relatively cool café and drank cold drinks slowly and with great pleasure. But the barman told me there was no inn in the village. For over an hour I tried to find a room but although I had much encouragement from the locals there was no accommodation to be had. It was too far to walk to the next village but, as I set out I was given a lift by a man who had earlier tried to be helpful.

I arrived in the town of Arrailos at the end of the afternoon. It was on a hill, white buildings perched on the sandy brown land. The people were friendly, the little streets picturesque, the main square spacious and quite grand but again there was no inn. Again I searched without success for a room and failed to find one.

At nine in the evening, I walked out of the town and minutes later was given a lift in an off-duty ambulance to the city of Evora, my next main objective.

It was very dispiriting to be ending the day in a vehicle, so as we drove south, I resolved to return the next morning to Arrailos by bus and travel to Evora on my own two feet.

At eight thirty next morning I was back in Arrailos, having breakfast in a small café, delighted that I had returned by bus to walk this section. It felt almost like a day off. The distance was shorter than usual. The day

Farm house in the Alentejo

would be hot but there was no sign yet of the enervating humidity. And now I had a room at an inn in Evora at the end of the walk.

I sipped my milky breakfast coffee and enjoyed the quiet bustle of the café. Attached to it was a small patisserie shop, whose wares were arranged with elegant style. To some, these delectable cakes might have seemed uncomfortably tempting. I had no such problem. From my table I could see the full display and had already decided on the half dozen of the toothsome confections I intended to take with me for nourishment on the way.

Having finished my rolls and honey, I selected an almond whorl, like a big Danish pastry, to have with a second cup of coffee. I had yet to stretch my legs properly but the day was starting off on the right foot.

I left the town with my box of cakes stowed carefully in my rucksac and kept looking back, the lovely white town set atop the skyline shining brilliantly in the morning sun.

My map showed a track across the hills to Evora and I called in the tiny post office, in the tiniest of villages, to check. The woman in charge shook her head and explained that there was no way through. She recommended the main road.

I thanked her and decided to try the track anyway. Five minutes later I heard a shout behind me. It was the woman from the post office. She took me firmly by the arm and led me back to the road. She shook her head vigorously from side to side and wagged a finger in front of my nose. I gathered that on no account was I to use the track. She made it clear in no uncertain terms that the road was good for walking, its surface even, shade at either side. Her brother was driving to Evora in half an hour and would give me a lift.

I smiled, declined the offer of a lift and thanked her for saving me from some unknown terror on that little track across the hills. She waited and watched to make sure I did not sneak back to the track as soon as her back was turned.

She was right about the road. It was shady and pleasant, with little traffic and great views across the countryside. The road rose and the views were even better, a baked landscape decorated with woods, olive groves, stands of peach trees and occasional white houses hiding behind the bushes.

It was the most leisurely day yet. I dandered along, spirits rising, singing to myself, playing an Irish jig tune with de-diddley-de-dee mouth music, stepping on or off the beat as I felt like it. The song was a sad air but then sad songs or sad poems have never depressed me. It is as if they let the soul make its own music, releasing sombre feelings if needs be.

This time I felt I had properly arrived in Evora, when I passed through the city walls and kept to the shady side of the streets. As I wandered to the centre a bird flopped down to the sunny pavement exhausted by the heat. A boy scooped it up and ran off to show it to his friends. My heart hoped that they would treat it kindly and let it go when recovered, but I saw a look of triumph on the boy's face, not concern, and my head told me otherwise.

Evora's charm is immediately obvious. It may be large but it seems compact, easily accessible. The Moorish influence is in its colour and shape, buildings of brightest white, marble in exquisite shades, tiled terraces and patios, balconies and archways shaped by Mohammedan art. It is the capital of the Alentejo, the great market of the province and the centre for its cork, wool and furniture industries.

For the first time, I was aware that there were other foreign visitors staying overnight. They were usually young, travelling by bus or train, pausing but briefly on their way. It was a surprise too, to hear occasional snatches of English spoken in the streets.

In the late afternoon I went to see the Roman Temple, remarkably well preserved and at the hub of Evora's historic sights. But, set here, amidst the medieval and Renaissance monuments, it seemed of a different age to the Roman remains which had so impressed me at Conimbriga.

Against my better judgement I visited the Casa dos Ossos, the Chapel of the Bones. Four hundred years ago a Franciscan monk covered its walls and pillars with the skulls and bones of thousands of his predecessors. The arrangement of bone on bone is precise, often to artistic effect, sometimes humorously so. At the entrance are braids hung by young women as ex-votos.

There are other chapels of bones in Europe, some touted merely as tourist attractions and perhaps grotesque. The first impression of the Casa dos Ossos in Evora is chilling, macabre, a stark reminder of the mortality of man. Some may come here and enjoy the gruesome but, for the rest of us, a moment of courage is required.

In a short space of time such a multitude of bones makes its own mark and we can accept our place amongst them, the privilege of being the living amongst the relics of those who once were too.

Unconsciously I touched, with my fingers and thumb, the bones of my own arm. The radius and the ulna moved easily together, thankfully they seemed alive, happily still within the flesh.

The chapel's Franciscan builder hoped his monumental work would encourage his fellow men to meditate. I found myself reflecting, without the least flicker of fear, about the finite nature of life's span.

Over the door there is an inscription, which can be translated as . . .
'We bones here are waiting for your bones'

Not a visit to be made on a bad day when the spirit is low. But now the melancholy of a few days before had gone. As I stepped out into the life of the street, I felt an inner strength, not the strength of physical power but the quiet vigour of the spirit that I would need to sustain me on the way.

Outside the day seemed bright and fresh, as if there had been a pause for reflection in the place of the dead. Now I was being welcomed back to the land of the living.

The town dog was asleep under the fountain. The pavement of one of the main streets was crowded with men, talking loudly and intensely absorbed in some important common purpose. Then I saw the election posters and understood. This was the hard core support for one of the parties of the left, about to show the strength of commitment.

Some of the men smiled when they saw me taking an interest. They shouted their slogans to me and offered me their leaflets. This was no fanatical group. There were men of all ages but no women that I could see, men of serious intent, determined to make the most of the opportunity to choose their rulers, now this was an option.

On the edge of the city a park merges into a huge open area, set aside for the Feira de São João, the great fair of St. John. It is the most important event in the year for the whole region. It lasts for ten days and I had, by chance, arrived in the middle of it.

In the evening, I strolled towards its sounds and found myself in the midst of a festival encampment as big as a small town. It was part exhibition, showing the history and crafts of the Alentejo, part market, with a huge variety of local products.

There were food stalls and restaurants by the dozen. A fun fair drew its own crowd of families, excitement rising by the minute. There were great displays of local pottery, brightly decorated, piled crock on crock. Stalls selling copper and brass kept their wares covered under awnings and were cleverly lit to make the metal jugs and bowls and ornaments gleam and flash, like treasures in a cave.

Folk groups in local costume wandered through the crowds, stopping to sing to anyone who would listen. There was an immense stage with full sound amplification for the main turns, mainly fada singers. The local radio was there, broadcasting live from the Fair.

I made my way to a building in the middle of the fair. This was the official restaurant, serving regional dishes prepared by local restaurants, which had been successful in a pre-fair competition. Admission was by ticket only and I had bought mine earlier in the day, at the tourist office.

The place was already half full and the customers were being entertained by a folk group of singers and musicians. Two girls in traditional costume met me at the door and showed me to a table. A Portuguese man was already there and, as he introduced himself as Angelo, the girls brought another guest, an American woman of great poise and charm called Luisha. Our table was complete when Nelson arrived later. He too was Portuguese and, like Angelo, spoke good English.

As far as I could see Luisha and I were the only foreigners in the room and the organisers had thoughtfully placed us with two men who could talk to us.

I could hardly believe it. Three companions for dinner who all spoke a language I could understand. It was such a shock to the system I was much quieter in company than I would usually expect to be. But there was no need for me to give a lead, Luisha was in charge. She was a very beautiful, self-assured woman, I thought in her mid-thirties, elegantly dressed in casual style and Angelo and Nelson were immediately smitten.

The food was delicious, shark soup to start with and then 'Carne de porco Alentejana', pork cooked in the Alentejo way but a different dish to the one I had tasted in Abrantes, more strongly flavoured with herbs. Angelo and Nelson insisted on buying the wine, one trying to outdo the other, to ensure we had the best local wine with the meal.

Luisha set us to guess each others ages. She and I put Angelo and Nelson down as in their mid-forties and that proved correct. They gallantly placed her at thirty, but trying to second guess her, and although she looked much younger, I tried forty. The two Portuguese looked at me in some annoyance, concerned at my lack of gallantry, but Luisha laughed and announced proudly that she was forty-four.

They were all kind when it came my turn, but although I was ten years older than the elder of the men, somehow I felt younger than either of them.

The conversation changed and the two men began to discuss something in Portuguese. Luisha looked thoughtful.

'Could a woman on her own make your kind of a journey?' It was a serious question, though she asked it in a deliberately casual, conversational tone. I smiled and told her about the travels of Freya Stark and Dervla Murphy.

I had met Freya Stark before my first climbing trip to Turkey and as she talked in her London flat, we might have been on one of her great journeys in the Middle-East.

Years later, when I took a mountaineering expedition to Afghanistan, the first question I was asked in that country was whether I knew

Dervla Murphy. It was a question needing no answer, such was the admiration of the Afghans for Dervla's cycle journey from Ireland to India. Coming from the same country, our standing as travellers was elevated to that of the highest order.

Luisha took a note of the names, so that she could read about the adventures of Freya and Dervla on her return home.

As she questioned me about making a journey like mine, I felt I had to say that the great helpfulness and friendship accorded to me might, in itself, present difficulties for a woman alone. Luisha agreed. Amongst such kindness might a woman not relax her guard? How would she know when helpfulness was a cover for some ulterior motive?

It was a dilemma I was not able to resolve for her. She saw my concern and smiled. Sometimes we try too hard to help when it is neither needed nor expected.

'You may be easy to recognise as a stranger.' she said. 'But what about me? I'm an obvious American tourist everywhere I go.' She laughed, easy in herself. She was coloured and her brown skin glowed with good-humoured pride. I had a feeling that wherever she travelled Luisha would always make good journeys.

The four of us parted at the door of the restaurant, at the end of a great evening. The food and music of the Alentejo had created its own special atmosphere and had proved to be a part of the Feira de São João not to be missed.

The town dog walked me home back to the heart of the city. He was a large, elderly off-white hound, a little over-weight, a little stiff in the joints. His usual place was a marble slab in the shade of the bowl of the fountain in the Praca do Giraldo.

He had obviously strolled down to the fair in the cool of the evening and I had seen him around the stalls, scuttling through the crowds, stiffness gone, enjoying the excitement and the stir like everyone else, picking up a few tit-bits here and there.

We kept each other company on the way back. I admired his style.

Some Portuguese towns give the impression that the internal combustion engine rules, that the car, the lorry, the motorbike take precedence over all. Evora's town dog allowed no such false presumption. He dandered across the street at his own pace, and when he felt like it. He relieved himself in the middle of the road when he needed to and the traffic had to steer around him. He paid not the slightest attention to blasting horns. Drivers even had do the unthinkable and use their brakes to stop, to let him pass.

That afternoon, I had watched him stir in his sleep as he lay full length on his marble slab. He wrinkled his nose and rose slowly to search for the source of the smell. It was a recently stubbed out cigarette, squashed to a brown smear on the pavement. He sniffed at it in disgust and walked back to his slab to continue his doze.

We talked to each other silently as we walked back and were friends by the time we reached the centre. He left me at the door of my hotel with a cheery look and ambled on home. We had both had a good evening out in his town and we knew it.

CHAPTER 13

Interlude in Lisbon

It was now four weeks since I had set out and I was due a break. Before leaving Lisbon for Santiago to begin my journey, I had been invited back for a tram ride around the old city, with members of the local St. Andrew's Society.

Lisbon was only a hundred miles away and next morning I skimmed through the countryside in the express coach, covering as much ground in a few hours, as I could walk in a week.

The tram ride around Lisbon was a great evening's entertainment. The St. Andrew's Society had booked two special coaches for the trip and there were fifty of us, mainly expatriates out for an evening on the town.

The sounds were from my childhood in Belfast, the clanging tram bell, the squeaking, grinding metal on metal of the wheels on the lines. I remembered hopping on the back platform as the tram slowed for the Monarch Laundry bend on the Donegall Road, but only when the conductor was upstairs collecting fares.

In Lisbon the wee boys were at the same trick. But here the yellow trams are still very much a part of the life of the city.

We had the traditional carriages, the only two still in use, velvet seats, upholstered ceilings, draped curtains at the windows with rows of little tassels, bobbing as we trundled along.

Jane, from the St Andrew's Society, had organised the outing and was our guide, and what a wonderful way to see the old town. We looked into lovely courtyards decked with pots of flowers and birds in cages. We passed an hotel which had been a monastery from the 16th century.

We followed the beautifully-named Street of the Green Windows and heard of the Streets of the Goldsmiths and the Silversmiths. A statue of a story teller in one district represents the great oral tradition of story telling in Portugal.

There are hills in the very heart of the city, one tram makes its run up and down a steep street like a funicular. We saw the street lift built by the engineer Eiffel, the elevador, and once his name is mentioned, it is easy to see the connection with his famous tower.

At dinner, in a little restaurant in the Alfalma quarter, I met my fellow passengers and, perhaps because they were interested in my journey, we seemed to find it easy to talk freely. We could confide in each other like old friends.

I heard of one man's work in a drug rehabilitation centre for young people in Scotland. In total contrast to the friendliness and honesty of the country districts, I was told of violent robbings, probably drug-related, in the most cosmopolitan of the tourist areas.

Another man, probably encouraged by me trying to explain how my journey seemed to release my inner thoughts, suddenly said,

'I died last year.' and shared his thoughts with me on the moments he had spent between life and death during a heart attack. His wife smiled her support and told me that they had never been happier than they were now. Every day was a special gift.

Like me in my short time in the country, these expatriates found the Portuguese people so friendly and helpful to live amongst. They talked of the warmth and the caring, loving atmosphere, a country where people count.

So much conversation, so many personal stories, but told in confidence and not to be broken here, enough to keep my mind busy on the last, long days of the walk.

Before I left Lisbon next morning, I went to see the Gulbenkian Collection. I had heard on the previous evening that it was not to be missed.

Calouste Gulbenkian was an Armenian oil trader who used his great wealth to acquire a magnificent collection of paintings, sculpture and historical artefacts. Before he died, he offered the countries of Europe the opportunity to bid for the right to provide a permanent home for the collection.

Portugal succeeded and the Gulbenkian Foundation built museums and concert halls on a site provided by the state in Lisbon. An orchestra was formed and the Foundation, in partnership with the state, makes a huge contribution to the cultural life of the country.

But it was Calouste Gulbenkian's own collection; now housed in one of the museums, which I wanted to see.

A visit to an art gallery requires great discipline. Usually there is so much to see, and in trying to see it all we may come away with only a vague impression of the whole. I try to restrict myself to seeing a few pictures only, in the hope that their images will stay with me.

One man's collection is a different matter. In Corfu, I had seen the works collected by a Greek diplomat during a lifetime of interest in the art of the East. I felt it let me see the character and personality of the man. It expressed his desires, his inner feelings, his obsessions, in a strangely lucid way, more evocative of the real man than photographs or biography. It had made more impression on me that some of the most famous paintings of the world.

But Gulbenkian's collection was on a different scale entirely. I started in the Egyptian Room with its myriad of pieces in stone, wood and gleaming metal, spectacularly displayed to evoke the epoch.

For two hours I wandered through a treasure house of the art of Greece and Rome, of China and the East, of Europe through the centuries.

The European art began with ivories and manuscripts and led me through an exquisite display of medals, tapestries and furniture to Rembrandt, Rubens, Turner and the Impressionists. The works by Gainsborough included an exceptionally beautiful portrait of a lady in a white wig and a blue gown.

Here were pictures that were world famous, Manet's 'Boy With Cherries', 'Madam Monet' painted by Renoir, landscapes by Corot, a drawing by Degas and three paintings by Monet himself, two of which, a still life and 'The Break-up Of The Ice', were painted at the very height of his career.

At the end of my visit, I came upon a specially designed room devoted to the jewellery and glass work of René Lalique in Art Nouveau style. Although some of the items were on loan elsewhere, there were enough pieces to show the skill and artfulness of this master jeweller. I found myself appreciating the art of jewellery for the first time.

Perhaps a month walking through the Portuguese countryside had cleared my mind for just such an experience. Some of the clutter had gone and left room for these magnificent images. My spirit was ready to appreciate them.

I left the Gulbenkian, in admiration of the man, not for his acquisition of such a treasure house but because, before his life had ended, he had made the effort to ensure that we could share it, in the fullness of its splendour.

CHAPTER 14

Revolution and Romance in the Alentejo

In the afternoon, I travelled back to Evora in style and next morning said good-by to my friend, the town dog, as I left the city, heading south.

The sky was open and blue, and the day was hot early. It was the last week of June and obvious that I would have the full heat of summer to contend with to the end of the walk.

My skin is fair and easily burned by the sun, but by now my arms, legs and face were brown. I had a bush hat with a large brim and a light scarf for the back of the neck, so I knew I could cope with the heat.

It was the humidity with the heat that I was dreading. Not only does it make the effort uncomfortable because the perspiration will not evaporate, keeping the skin of the whole body in a sweaty, sticky state, but it also saps the energy and the will to keep going. I had been told the Alentejo would be hot and dry but the experience of a few days before had proved that this was not always the case.

Four boys, standing up in a cart like Roman soldiers, whipped their mule to make him trot up the hill into the town.

There was no alternative but to follow the road to Viana do Alentejo. There were so few vehicles it was a pleasant walk, the road shaded on one side, cutting a straight swathe through fields of wheat, forests of cork oak, obviously following the line of the ancient track between the settlements.

The traffic was so light, I felt that walking the roads in the north of Ireland must have been like this forty years ago, although there are parts of the island where it would still be the case.

A great lorry lumbered past, laden with the bark of the cork oak, heading for the processing factory, the driver waving to me. The bark is held down by steel cables and, as the load settles, the driver will have to stop to tighten the grip of the cables on the load.

The humidity rose in the afternoon and, as it did so, the pleasure of the walk began to fade. Viana do Alentejo is well away from the main road south. It was once fortified and its castle walls and towers, with their pepperpot roofs are still a spectacular landmark.

The town was dusty and dry, white-shuttered houses and silent streets. I could only hope that I would find a room and a meal, for this was far enough for the day.

By now, I felt I had walked back into Portugal's past. It was as if the long days of travelling slowly through the countryside had somehow let me make contact with the country, not in terms of knowledge but somehow in touch with the essence of the land.

Every country is a captive of its own history – Portugal's past had created a state powerfully influenced by its invaders and developed by the enterprise of its own military and merchant adventurers. It is a nation apart in its own corner of Iberia, separate from Spain, its larger neighbour, in temperament, language and culture.

In the centuries before the Christian era, the Greeks and Phoenicians established trading posts on its coasts. The Romans and the Visigoths came in their turn, the former leaving fine monuments to their stay and both their distinctive marks on the land.

The Moors left their shapes and forms on the towns and villages and traces of their style with the people.

The Church became paramount after the Reconquest of the country from the Moors and this is still evident in the wealth of architecture which developed from that period. At one time, the city of Braga, in the north, was the seat of the Primate of all Iberia.

By the 14th century, Portugal had achieved the status of a country. There were wars with Spain and a period of domination by that state.

The Anglo-Portuguese Alliance dates back to this era and at a time of crises during World War 2, Winston Churchill named Portugal as Britain's oldest ally.

In medieval times, the famous Voyages of Discovery led to a vast colonial empire. Prince Henry the Navigator used huge resources in its development. Vasco da Gama opened the sea route to India. The burgeoning trade brought prosperity and wealth on a grand scale. When da Gama brought back a small cargo of pepper from one of his voyages, it raised more than three times the cost of his expedition.

The established trade to Africa and the East allowed Portugal to continue to prosper through the centuries.

When France invaded, at the beginning of the 19th century, General Wellesley, who later became the Duke of Wellington, was sent from England and led his troops to victory in the Peninsular Campaign.

When a country prospers, there is no guarantee that the resulting wealth will be shared. The rich may grow wealthier and the poor remain tied to a level of subsistence which generates anger and envy.

At the beginning of the 20th century Portugal became a Republic and, after years of instability, a Professor of Economics, Dr Salazar came to power. For nearly forty years, until 1968, he ruled with authoritarian control. An economic infrastructure was established but few benefited and, in particular, agriculture remained underdeveloped.

In 1974 the Armed Forces seized power to popular acclaim and soldiers entered Lisbon with red carnations in the muzzles of their rifles. The Government was swept aside and the new Portugal emerged. This was the Revolution of the 25th April and the next few years produced a dramatic process of change.

Banking and private insurance companies were nationalised. Property and land were seized from the wealthy. Portuguese colonies in Africa were given their independence. Estates were taken over by the farmworkers and co-operatives were formed to work the land and sell the products.

Although it had all happened thirteen years before, here, in the Alentejo, the events of the 25th April 1974 were commemorated everywhere.

The Revolution changed the whole country, but it was in the Alentejo that its most profound effects on farming were felt. In the north, the land holdings were usually small, so small they could only provide subsistence. In the south, the farms were vast, usually owned by one family, worked by peasants in a strictly feudal structure that was sometimes benign, even responsible. However, the workers felt exploited by the landowners and the system.

Taking over the estates and running them as collectives seemed the obvious answer to the problems of poverty in the Alentejo. In the event, a lack of finance to see the new enterprises through a succession of poor harvests, ensured that earning a living wage was more difficult than ever.

Some farms have been bought back by the former owners and new landowners, some from abroad, have been drawn to this land. The remaining collectives have benefited by government help and the situation is improving. As the states of Europe come together, it may well be that a country like Portugal will have most to gain.

Now, and for the first time since I had entered the country, I felt I was truly amongst the changes wrought by the revolution. I had been told to be wary, that strangers were not necessarily welcome in all the towns and villages. But for me, on foot, the friendly reception was just as I had become accustomed to, since I entered the country.

There was no inn in Viana but I found a comfortable room in a house and had my evening meal in a bar. I was away much earlier than usual next morning. The only cool part of the day was first thing and, as I left the town, work was beginning in the countryside.

Politics in the Alentejo

The plantations of cork oaks were carefully managed. To give the trees the best chance of using any moisture in the land, they were well spaced and the ground between them kept free of weeds.

The trees are pollarded, the main trunks cut to encourage the thick growth of lateral branches, thus making the stripping of the bark easier. When it is being harvested the bark is completely removed to head height or higher and the tree left for years to recover.

I walked a road like that of the previous day, but this time through orange groves and olive groves, as well as great plains of wheat.

A group of gipsies were camped at the roadside with five young mules, making the best of the grazing on the verge. The gipsies waved and called to me but I understood not one word. The shouts seemed to be in a different language I had never heard before.

After three or four hours I reached a quiet village and found a bar. Stepping inside out of the burning heat was sweet relief. The bar was spacious and cool and the proprietor was standing on tip-toes on a high stool carefully dusting the television. His back was to me and, although he must have heard my entrance, he made no acknowledgement of it, thinking it was one of the locals.

Then he turned and, seeing a stranger in his establishment, jumped down and came over to shake hands with me. He spoke a little English and we talked about making a living in this sun-baked land.

I asked him if Portugal was a better place, a fairer country, since the Revolution.

'It depends who you ask.' he said 'In this village the workers are sure it is. But they have to believe that. It is their only hope.' He smiled, at ease in himself although he was talking politics, as if he knew it was safe to talk to me.

'Go to Cuba.' he said with a grin, 'See for yourself.'

Cuba was the next town on my road. Had it given its name to that famous Caribbean island? My first thought was that its traditional name had been changed to that of Fidel Castro's republic, to mark the Alentejo's own red revolution. Then that seemed far too plausible an explanation to be credible. It was easier to believe in the irony of this place being so named, when communism became such a force in this region.

There were few people about, as if the population was all at work at this time of the day. The town had an air of industry, there was a huge granary, factories, a railway station. On the way in, the cork oak and olive plantations and the farms had looked particularly well-cared for. It was not that the town seemed so prosperous, but it was unobtrusively busy, earnestly industrious. Walking through, it was easy to believe that the Revolution was working here.

I was heading for Beja, but it was too far after so long in the heat and humidity. I stopped at a village and waited for a bus.

Beja was on high ground overlooking a huge stretch of plains. A thunder shower cleared the air and the town was much fresher than Evora. There was much less traffic noise too, fewer blaring car horns and, to my amazement, most of the motorbikes had silencers!

I found an inn without trouble and stood under a cold shower for twenty minutes, to cool the burning heat in my head, neck and back.

The town is built to keep the searing heat of the plains at bay, its shady streets angled to catch the cool airs. When I was sufficiently recovered, I explored the town and found the Convento de Nostra Senora da Conceição, the Convent of the Conception. The Convent is now a museum but remains at the very heart of one of the great romantic mysteries of European literature.

I was just in time, the last one allowed in at the end of the afternoon session. Although I seemed to be the only visitor, no one hurried me in order to close the place for the day. I had time to sit in the chapel, surrounded by its images. The woodwork was intricately carved, gilded, but more appealing to me when I could see the line and grain of the wood itself.

The chapterhouse is decorated with beautiful Moorish azulejos, as fine as can be found in the whole of the country.

Upstairs, there is the reconstruction of the grilled window of the nun's cell, through which the first passes of the famous love story were enacted.

In the 17th century, a Poor Clare nun, Sister Mariana Alcoforado and a French cavalry officer, Count Chamilly, are said to have fallen in love. They wrote to each other, they whispered through the grill. Then the Count had to return to France at the end of the War of Devolution and the lovers were parted, never to meet again.

A year later, five love letters written by Mariana, were published in a French translation in Paris. Versions in Portuguese and English were produced and the letters were soon famous. They spoke in the language of love, of passion and despair, of urgency and entreaty. The letters became classics of romantic literature.

Such was the quality of the translation in French however, that scholars were soon questioning the authenticity of the letters. The originals were never produced and, although the nun and the soldier existed and were both in Beja at the time, the mystery of the love story remains unsolved.

The next two days passed in a blur of golden wheat shining in the brightest sunlight with blessed shade when I reached a cork oak plantation. I tried to hide from the sun under my big hat and behind sunglasses. For miles I followed an old path beside the road. It was dustier than the surfaced highway, but led me through the trees when I reached a forest.

The terrain was undulating and far more beautiful than I had been led to expect. Some of the guide books dismissed it as 'dull' and 'staggeringly monotonous'. But then travelling at speed, as the car or coach cuts down the scale of the Alentejo and makes the towns seem closer than they are, is to miss the very nature of the place. Only my friend Caroline spoke up for this country. She loved it and had prepared me for its grandeur.

Certainly it is a harsh land, sparsely populated, the soil often poor, lacking rainfall, and at this time of year, exceedingly hot. Winning a living from the soil must be hard, but little of the land is left fallow.

Here are yellow blooms amongst the plantations of olives, cork oak, oranges, figs, great expanses of wheat. White villages with their orchards and groves of trees are scattered far apart on quiet roads, with blooms of brightest white, blue and red along their verges .

It creates a magnificently spacious landscape, ordered without appearing to be so, like no other part of Iberia. It shimmers in the baking heat, warm tints of gold, shades of green promising relief, flashes of brilliant colour glowing, vast and splendidly beautiful.

It was hard walking country too, tough going in the humid heat, but never 'dull' or 'monotonous', not for one step of the way.

On the road to Vale de Añor I saw ten combine harvesters, in echelon, one just behind the other, harvesting the wheat in a field that looked as big as an Irish county. Every one of the drivers waved to me and the tiredness fell away. In some unreasoned way it was a proud moment when these men recognised me, as if, instinctively, they knew about my journey.

There was no inn in Vale de Añor and it was even harder to find a room. A few enquiries led me to a private house, and again I had a simple meal in a bar and a restful night.

On the way to Mertola in the morning, I walked through a forest for hours. The route rose through a range of low hills with swathes of wild flowers in full bloom beside the almost dry beds of streams. In another month the streams will cease to flow, but many of the plants have hard, shiny, spiky leaves and are adapted for the drought to come.

I always warn walkers, when they are contemplating holiday routes in this kind of terrain in Southern Europe, to keep to the paths. Walking across country is not like striding through heather or across the fells. The plants protect themselves by striking at the ankles and calves with

Azulejos

vicious barbs. They mean us no harm, but survival requires that they defend themselves.

There was one small village on my route but no people, nor any sign of a bar or café. Now I could value the two litres of water I was carrying, which, in the relative cool of the morning, I resented because of the weight. I kept going all day with the briefest of pauses. Then I crossed a ridge and saw the white town of Mertola below me, perched on a little hill on the western bank of the Rio Guadiana.

The Guadiana was the last great river of Portugal I hoped to cross, but not yet. I was due to follow it south and make the crossing at its mouth, as it ended its journey by reaching the Gulf of Cadiz, and I ended mine by leaving Portugal to finish in Spain.

The struggle of the past two days washed away under the shower in the inn at Mertola. It left me tired, but easy in myself. It was thirty days since I had set out from Santiago and there was a deeper weariness under the fatigue of the day. I could accept that. It was only to be expected.

This is the time when mind over matter is important. Physical tiredness, even a degree of exhaustion, may be coped with if the spirits are high. The difficult moments of life, when stress is at its most unbearable, often happen when we are already trying to cope with other problems. There could be extreme physical tiredness, compounded by lack of sleep, ailments like headache, stomach upset, hypertension, panic attack. This is the time when we need to call on the inner strength.

But this was not that kind of difficult time for me. I was merely tired physically, very tired. I had a bed and a meal arranged, and my inner strength felt more powerful than ever. So I sat on the terrace of the Central Café, at the corner of the road, to watch the afternoon life of Mertola pass by and allow myself the luxury of feeling tired.

Rested and refreshed, I stirred myself and took a stroll. The whitewashed church above the river was once a mosque. The arches are Moorish and the mihrab, the Imam's prayer niche, is still in place behind the altar. The locals believe that this is the only former mosque in Portugal where the mihrab and the Islamic columns and arches can still be admired.

In the times of the Moors, Mertola was the capital of a small kingdom within the Arab domain. On a height above it is the ruin of the castle, now being excavated. The view from the walls is spectacular, along the river, across the undulating land, and south to the Serra do Caldeirão. This is the range which separates the Alentejo from the Algarve coast, the hills I would have to cross to reach the Azure Ocean.

I was back on the raised terrace of the café in a grandstand seat for the

The Moorish castle on the hill

excitement of the evening rush hour. A policeman appeared in a grand uniform, with gold braid and a whistle hanging from a white lanyard on one shoulder. He conducted the traffic in nonchalant style, pointing with his baton, giving a sharp blast of the whistle for dramatic effect and, only occasionally, showing a flash of annoyance. The performance must have lasted for all of twenty minutes and then, duty done for the day, he strolled over to have a cool drink at the café.

A short distance away there was a restaurant. It looked unpretentious, even a little down-at-heel. But, from my first day in this country, I had learned that the appearance of an eating place was no guide to its food. I had a feeling too, that this might be my last chance of a good meal before I reached journey's end. I was not disappointed.

As I sat down, a bowl of pigs ears and a jug of cool white wine were placed on the table. The pigs ears are cooked in garlic and coriander and are a favourite appetiser in the Alentejo. It was a good start.

My main course was 'Borrego assado no forno', lamb baked in a casserole. That afternoon, in the searing heat, I had doubted that I would be able to manage more than a snack in the evening, but it was different now. I felt recovered and hungry enough to do justice to a real meal.

The lamb was served in one of the local pottery dishes, still sizzling as it was placed on the table, too hot to eat, but then I was in no hurry. I drank a glass of the wine and dipped a piece of bread in the dish to taste the sauce. It was delicious. The girl who was serving saw that I approved and smiled.

I waited for the dish to cool and enjoyed it in its own good time. This was the proper pace for a meal, time to taste and appreciate, time to feel the atmosphere of the place, time to savour the Alentejo at its hospitable best.

On the way out of Mertola in the morning, a shepherd and his huge flock of sheep and goats had taken full rights of passage on the road. It presented no problem for me. I simply climbed a bank at the road side and waited until they had passed.

For once the internal combustion engine had to give way. Traffic coming in the opposite direction had to wait. Traffic travelling in the same direction as the flock had to follow behind, at the pace of the slowest sheep. For them, there was no way past. I sat on the bank and enjoyed the triumph of the old ways over the new.

The road climbed above a river and I came upon a group of women washing clothes, in what was obviously the traditional place. There were flat stones for pounding the garments and pools for rinsing. Their big wicker baskets were on the bank, piled high with more items for the wash. But there was no sign of habitation nearby. Although I was on a vantage point, I could see no village, not even a single house.

I walked on for an hour, puzzled about the siting of the wash place, without any sign of where the washerwomen might live.

Alamo was the village of the friendly dogs. They were either very small terriers or large hounds, no middle-sized mongrels here. The small dogs were for for herding or kept as pets but I had a feeling that the big dogs were for hunting or still used to guard the flocks.

It seemed even hotter in the afternoon and even more humid than usual. The road wound through the hills, and needing a rest, I sat down in the shade for a drink of water. There was no traffic and out of the still of the afternoon came two mounted policemen, like actors in a period film.

From my seat the horses looked enormous, walking with slow, deliberate strides, full of power, prancing a few steps to show it. The men were in ornate, immaculate uniforms and chatting as they rode. They must have seen me but they made no acknowledgement of my presence. Even my greeting went unanswered. It was the first time since I had entered Portugal that I had been totally ignored.

I reached the little village of Espirito Santo but there was no inn, nor was there a room to be found. I walked on and somewhere here amongst the hills, I left the Alentejo and crossed the provincial border into the Algarve.

There was no feeling of elation, only disappointment, for now I knew I had to look for a lift back to Mertola to spend the night.

Next morning, I took a bus back to where I had finished the previous evening and, for the first time felt a sense of urgency. If all went well, the next day would be my last.

I was now amongst the hills and climbing in beautiful terrain, rugged, rocky slopes, wild growth of trees and bushes, carpets of flowers, no ordered planting here. This was a terrain as ordained by nature, not man.

Two cars stopped to offer lifts and the drivers were surprised when I politely declined. I met a gang of men repairing the road. The foreman stood in the shade of a tree, watching their every move. The men were in distinctive uniforms, every one hard at work. Were they convicts serving hard-labour sentences?

In the middle of the afternoon, in the sizzling heat, I reached the village of Odeleite. There was no inn, but I found a room and a simple meal in a house nearby. It was no discomfort, I could happily have slept in a shed and dined on bread and cheese. To-morrow I would see the sea.

CHAPTER 15

The Last Stage to the Azure Ocean

It was hot early and I climbed steadily amongst the hills. This was real mountain country, the Serra do Caldeirão, and pleasant walking in spite of the rising heat. The sole of my shoe was beginning to look like parting company again from the upper.

In the middle of the morning I crossed the ridge and saw the sea. It was a moment of exultation. The deep, underlying tiredness of the journey eased. My back straightened. The pack felt lighter. I stopped worrying about the errant sole of my shoe. I whooped aloud, not loud enough to frighten the wild life, of course, but my body needed to let my spirits know that the end was now in sight.

The sea was the greyish blue of the Atlantic Ocean seen from above and still a long way off. Just the colour that had been in my mind's eye for the past five weeks. The blue would deepen, of course, as I approached, until, close to, it reached its true azure hue.

It was all downhill now, no hurry, only a matter of four hours or so and I should be strolling into Vila Real de Santo Antonio at the mouth of the Rio Guadiana.

Almost at once, I felt a cool breeze gently wafting up the slope – the first cool air I could remember for twenty days. There were even clouds in the sky. Idyllic walking weather – was it a reward on the last day for struggling so long in the heat?

Another region of Portugal stretched in front of me and reminded me that each one thus far had been so different from the others, they might have been separate countries.

When, at the start of the journey, I crossed the Rio Minho into the mountains of the north, it had rained as much as I would have expected at home in Ireland. The vegetation was dense, the forests of pine and eucalyptus vast. There were small farms with granite fence posts and vines on racks at head height. There were apple orchards and olive groves and fields of turnips grown for their tops.

I had visited Braga and Guimarães, the old cities of Portugal, and found the ancient Celtic village of Briteiros perched on a hill. I had crossed my second great river, the beautiful Rio Lima, the mythical Roman River of Oblivion.

Then I reached the Rio Douro, the River of Gold, and crossed it at the great modern city of Porto, the home of the world-famous port wine trade.

My route had taken me south along the coast into the Beira Region. Seemingly endless beaches and miles of sand dunes led me to the fishing village, where the chain of help for the stranger with the lost sole, had given me new hope for the humanity of man. The small seaside holiday towns were quiet, although it was the month of June. They seemed used exclusively, as yet, by the Portuguese and, at this time of year, at week-ends only.

There were sheltered lagoons and huge areas of irrigated land, rice fields, vine yards, forests of pine on the sand.

When I left the coast and turned inland towards the heart of the country, I was in the Ribatejo, the region of the River Tagus. There I found the magnificent castle of the Templar Knights at Tomar and sat bemused with their ghosts in their inner sanctum.

Below the hills were the rich, easily irrigated plains, along the banks of the river. There were rice fields, vines, olives, fruit orchards and market gardens. In the great meadows of the province, the famed horses and black fighting bulls of the Ribatejo are reared.

Then I crossed the Tagus into the huge plains of the Alentejo, an immense province, covering nearly a third of the country. There was virtually no natural vegetation, except on the ridges and amongst the hills of the south.

The land is dry, the summers hot, but water drawn from deep wells by wind power or donkey power, irrigates vast fields of wheat and cork oak plantations. Peaches and oranges grow in abundance. There are ancient towns and villages, many decorated with azulejos, the beautiful, coloured Moorish tiles.

Here were the finest mules I have ever seen, sturdy, strong, well-cared for and so biddable they could undermine that grand animal's reputation for stubbornness.

It took me two weeks to travel the length of the Alentejo, and now I had left that province for the Algarve. It is the best known of all the regions of Portugal, because of its popularity as a holiday destination. But such fame can carry with it the seeds of its own desolation.

This was my first visit and, although one of the guide books describes some of the holiday developments along the coast as 'pretty grim', I had heard that this was a relaxed place, popular with the Portuguese as well as foreigners. It was said, too, that there were unspoilt beaches, picturesque villages, and friendly, charming towns.

The miles passed as I re-lived the journey in my mind. It was strange to be on such a long downhill stretch, the terrain carrying me with it, without the usual effort.

I was in no hurry to get the last day over. It was not like climbing a high mountain. Once the summit is reached, there is a great sense of relief that the struggle upwards is over at last. The view, and the ecstasy of rest, have to wait until the needs of survival have been attended to – water to drink – something to eat – a look at the route of descent. The sense of achievement, if any, has to wait. The climb is only half over at the top. Ascent must be followed by descent. There will be time enough for celebration at the mountain's foot.

A journey like this creates its own pace. The time scale is vastly longer than that of a climb. The risks are different. There is time to absorb and appreciate the experience, as it happens. However, although the hazards are different, many of the principles of survival and travel in unfamiliar terrain are the same.

The route of a walk such as mine, like the mountain climb, is as it is, not necessarily an ideal walking or climbing environment. To appreciate the nature of the country is to travel with the land, following its grain, like selecting the line of least resistance on the climb.

Throughout this trip there had been time to linger, but on this day time seemed of no consequence and I paused in every village for a coffee and a cool drink.

In the village of Castro Marin, the beautiful church was plastered with election posters, demanding votes for the CDU, the United Democratic Coalition, formed specially for this election, as an alliance between the parties of the communists and the ecologists.

It seemed like a defiant gesture to choose such a poster site. The Revolution produced conflict between the Church and the workers. An Archbishop had pronounced on the struggle against communism as being ' not in terms of man against man, but Christ against Satan'. In villages, I had seen small shrines defaced. Attempts had been made to restore some, but not all, and they remained a poignant reminder of the turmoil of that time.

The last four kilometres seemed longer than they should have been. The land was flat, intensively cultivated, with an occasional patch of derelict sheds and machinery, as if a holding had failed. The bushes were on fire along one side of the road and for two or three minutes I had to walk through the smoke. The fire was being watched by workmen and I suspected that it had been started deliberately, to clear the undergrowth.

Vila Real de Santo Antonio was impressive, the buildings a blend of the old and the new. It had the holiday air of a resort, freshly decorated,

spruce and bright at the beginning of the season. There were no huge concrete hotels nor any sign of the excesses of package tourism. Its atmosphere was happy and relaxed, charming, friendly in a rather dignified way.

I walked its streets and came upon a paved pedestrian area which led to the great square. There were family groups and couples enjoying the shops, keeping the cafés busy, making room for others to pass, as they strolled.

An old man approached, dressed immaculately in a black suit and hat, white shirt, polished black shoes. He leant heavily on a stick, bent double, his head on the same level as his waist.

A few yards behind came a second old man, also well-dressed, frail, sight failing, tapping the ground with his stick four or five times before making each step, feeling his way along the fine mosaic tiles. Even the snail I had met on my first day, leaving Santiago, would have left him behind. But this walk along the street was his challenge. He would make it, and in his own time. It put in perspective any sense of achievement I felt I might be entitled to.

The leg-weariness of the walk suddenly seemed of no consequence. I greeted each of the men as he passed. The one bent double turned his head and smiled up at me, as he returned my word. The other paused in his tapping and gave me a happy little bow in acknowledgement.

The great square is surrounded by orange trees and paved with black and white tiles, in a mosaic radiating from its central monument. The houses around its sides are of the same epoch, elegant architecture, set off by wrought-iron balconies and decorative balustrades.

I watched a bride and groom pose for their wedding photographs between the orange trees, the bride in white and the groom in black to match the mosaic tiles. A folk singer was perched on the plinth of the monument, singing international folk songs to a crowd of young people.

I reached the Rio Guadiana, its bank landscaped with gardens and an esplanade, pointing the town across the estuary towards Spain. The sea was on my right, meeting the river at its mouth. Across the great width of the estuary, the white town of Ayamonte sat snugly into the land.

Vila Real de Santo Antonio is a proper frontier town, a resort and a harbour. A tidal wave had destroyed the former settlement and in the 18th century the new town was designed by the Marques de Pombal. It was built in a matter of months to a grid pattern, modelled on the Baxia quarter of Lisbon.

I sat down on an esplanade seat and looked across at Spain and down stream to the sea. Having left the Pilgrim City in the north, the Azure Ocean of the south was now in view.

It seemed that the journey was reaching its natural end. The soles of my sturdy walking shoes had worn thin and one was again in the process of detaching itself. My once-brick-red rucksac was now frayed and faded to dustiest pink. My legs and feet felt they had walked enough. It must be a good time to stop.

I booked a room and left my rucksac in a tiny hotel above a bank on the other side of the esplanade. I took the ferry across the Guadiana to Spain. Later in the summer the service is so popular that there are queues to board the boat for Spain – but not on this day. The little ship was pleasantly full and headed purposefully up-stream, steering a diagonal course to allow for the strength of the current.

It was my last great river of Portugal and I leaned over the rail on the port side, looking back along the way I had come. I sketched Castro Marin on its little hill and saw behind it the mountains which separated the Alentejo from the Algarve.

It all looked so far away, but it felt even further back in time, as if I had crossed those hills weeks ago, not yesterday.

I had one small coin from home left and I dropped it over the side into the Guadiana. Again it felt like an offering to the gods, a token of privilege for being here.

I stepped off the boat at Ayamonte and found a tree-shaded square amongst its quiet, afternoon streets. It seemed like siesta time and it was certainly Spain, not Portugal. The buildings, the voices, the food smells, the atmosphere, even the bird song seemed different.

I sat down on a wooden seat in the shade of the trees and knew that this was the end of my journey. Five weeks before, I had started in Santiago de Compostela in the north of Spain, where I had finished my journey along the pilgrim Road to Santiago two years before. That experience had started as a walk and become a pilgrimage.

Now I was disinclined to differentiate. Life's journey is its own pilgrimage. This time, I had crossed the rivers of Portugal and travelled the length of that great country, to finish my journey back in Spain.

I made myself no promises, as I sat on the seat in Ayamonte, but did wonder if I would come back to this spot some day and continue walking around Iberia. When I reached Santiago, I felt that the arrival in the Pilgrim City was a new beginning, not an end. Now, the thought of returning here to start again, seemed like a good idea. But this was no time to be making plans for the future. I had to get back on the ferry to celebrate the crossing of the rivers of Portugal with the choicest food and wine that Vila Real could provide.

It is best to travel on one journey at a time.

ALSO BY THE SAME AUTHOR

PILGRIMS' FOOTSTEPS – first published by Quest Books in 1989. In 1985 Bert Slader set out on his own to walk the 1,000-year-old pilgrim road to Santiago de Compostela in N-W Spain. In PILGRIMS' FOOTSTEPS he recounts the experiences of that journey, telling the stories of the places and the people and reflecting on the inner journey of his thoughts.

There is an Appendix on the country cooking of Northern Spain with recipes for regional dishes and an Information Section for those who wish to make the journey on foot or by car.

Reprint available July 1991 from bookshops @ £6.50
Signed copies available direct from Quest Books (NI) @ £6.50 or IR£7.00 (see below for details)

PILGRIMS' FOOTSTEPS TAPE A 90 minute audio tape of stories from Pilgrims' Footsteps, narrated by the author. Available direct from Quest Books (NI) @ £6.50 or IR£7.00 including postage(see below for details)

BEYOND THE BLACK MOUNTAIN, first published July 1990, is set in Ulster during the years 1939 to 1946. It tells a story of growing up during the war in West Belfast and the experiences which encouraged the young Bert Slader to travel. It relates the adventures of his cycle journey around the Province, with an even younger companion, in the days of strict food rationing and austerity.

Bert links the journey with later experiences in other lands. He reflects on the sectarian allegiances and religious beliefs of the time and the effect of these divisions on the growing generation.

Reprinted October 1990. Illustrations by Wilfrid Capper.

Available from bookshops @ £4:95.
Signed copies available direct from Quest Books (NI) @ £4:95 or IR£5:40 (see below for details)

For signed copies of the books or the tape write to:

Quest Books (NI), 2 Slievenabrock Ave, Newcastle, Co. Down, N. Ireland BT33 0HZ.

Please add towards postage and packing 55p per book for UK and IR£1.00 for Rep. of Ireland.

Tape postage free.